Contents

CHOCOLATE BROWNIES

Makes 16 brownies

PREP TIME: 10 minutes
CHILLING TIME: 3 hours
EQIPMENT: 9-inch square baking pan

Ingredients:

- Nonstick baking spray
- 1 (14-ounce) can sweetened condensed milk
- 2 ounces unsweetened chocolate, finely chopped
- 2½ cups graham cracker crumbs

Directions:

1. Spray a 9-inch square baking pan with baking spray.
2. In a medium saucepan set over medium-low heat, combine the sweetened condensed milk and chocolate. Cook for about 10 minutes, stirring constantly, until the chocolate is completely melted and the mixture is smooth. Remove the pan from the heat.
3. Add the graham cracker crumbs to the saucepan and stir to mix well. Transfer the mixture to the prepared baking pan and spread it into an even layer. Place the pan in the refrigerator and chill for at least 3 hours until well set. Slice into bars and serve chilled or refrigerate, covered, for up to 1 week.

SALTED CARAMEL–STUFFED FUDGE BROWNIES

Makes about 24 brownies

PREP TIME: 10 minutes
COOK TIME: 47 to 52 minutes
EQIPMENT: 9-by-13-inch baking pan

Ingredients:

- Nonstick baking spray
- 1½ cups all-purpose flour
- 1 teaspoon salt
- 1 teaspoon baking powder
- 2 cups sugar
- ¾ cup unsweetened cocoa powder
- 1 cup neutral-flavored oil (such as grapeseed, safflower, or sunflower seed)
- 4 eggs
- ¼ cup low-fat or whole milk
- 1 cup (6 ounces) semisweet chocolate chips
- 1 (11-ounce) package caramels or caramel pieces (such as Kraft Vanilla Caramels or Kraft Caramel Bits)

- 1 (14-ounce) can sweetened condensed milk
- 1 teaspoon coarse sea salt

Directions:

1. Preheat the oven to 350°F.
2. Line a 9-by-13-inch baking pan with parchment paper, and spray the parchment with baking spray.
3. In a medium bowl, stir together the flour, salt, and baking powder.
4. In a large bowl, with a wooden spoon or electric mixer, mix the sugar, cocoa powder, oil, eggs, and milk until well combined and smooth.
5. Add the flour mixture and stir or beat until incorporated.
6. Stir in the chocolate chips. Spoon ⅔ of the batter into the prepared pan and bake for 12 minutes.
7. Meanwhile, in a medium microwave-safe bowl, combine the caramels and sweetened condensed milk. Microwave at 50 percent power, in 30-second intervals, until the caramel melts and the mixture is smooth.
8. Remove the partially baked brownies from the oven and pour the melted caramel mixture over the top, spreading it into an even layer. Sprinkle the coarse sea salt over the caramel and then drop the remaining brownie batter on top in heaping spoonfuls. Using a butter knife, gently swirl together the caramel and brownie mixtures. Return to the oven and bake for 35 to 40 minutes more, until set and a toothpick inserted into the center comes out clean.
9. Remove from the oven and let the brownies cool completely before slicing and serving. Store in an airtight container at room temperature for up to 1 week.

BROWN SUGAR AND BUTTERSCOTCH BLONDIES

Makes about 16 blondies

PREP TIME: 5 minutes

COOK TIME: 25 to 30 minutes

EQIPMENT: 8-inch square baking pan

Ingredients:

- ½ cup (1 stick) unsalted butter, melted, plus more for preparing the baking pan
- 1 cup packed dark brown sugar
- 1 egg, lightly beaten
- 1 teaspoon vanilla extract
- 1 cup all-purpose flour
- ½ teaspoon baking powder
- ⅛ teaspoon baking soda
- Pinch salt
- ⅓ cup butterscotch chips

Directions:

1. Preheat the oven to 350°F.
2. Generously grease an 8-inch square baking pan with butter.
3. In a large bowl, whisk the melted butter with the brown sugar.

4. Whisk in the egg and vanilla.

5. Add the flour, baking powder, baking soda, and salt, and mix to combine.

6. Stir in the butterscotch chips. Transfer the batter to the prepared pan and spread into an even layer. Bake for 25 to 30 minutes, until a toothpick inserted into the center comes out clean.

7. Remove from the oven and let the blondies cool before cutting into bars and serving. Store in an airtight container at room temperature for up to 1 week.

CANDY-COATED POPCORN

Makes 10 cups

PREP TIME: 5 minutes
COOKING TIME: 5 minutes
SETTING TIME: 30 minutes
EQIPMENT: Medium saucepan
Ingredients:

- 10 cups popped popcorn (from about ⅔ cup kernels) or 1 to 2 bags microwave popcorn
- ½ cup (1 stick) unsalted butter
- ⅔ cup sugar
- ⅓ cup corn syrup
- 1 teaspoon vanilla extract
- Food coloring (optional)

Directions:

1. Place the popcorn in a large bowl and set aside.

2. In a medium saucepan set over medium heat, stir together the butter, sugar, corn syrup, and vanilla until the butter and sugar completely dissolve. Bring to a boil. Remove from the heat and stir in the food coloring (if using).

3. Pour the mixture over the popcorn and toss to coat well. Let cool for about 30 minutes. Serve immediately or store in an airtight container at room temperature for up to 1 week.

RAINBOW ROCK CANDY

Makes about 30 pieces

PREP TIME: 5 minutes
COOK TIME: 30 minutes
EQIPMENT: Baking sheet, candy thermometer (recommended, but not required)
Ingredients:

- Nonstick baking spray
- 2 cups sugar
- ½ cup light corn syrup
- ½ teaspoon flavoring oil of your choice
- Food coloring, for coloring the candies
- Powdered sugar, for dusting

Directions:

1. Coat a baking sheet with nonstick bak

1. ing spray.

2. In a large saucepan set over medium-high heat, stir together the sugar, corn syrup, and ½ cup water. Bring to a boil. Cook for 20 to 30 minutes. If using a candy thermometer, cook the mixture until it reaches 300°F. If you are not using a candy thermometer, test the temperature by dropping a teaspoon or so of the mixture into a glass of ice water. When it is up to temperature, it will harden and become crunchy immediately.

3. Remove the pan from the heat and add the flavoring oil and food coloring as desired. You can split this mixture into batches and add different flavors and colors to each batch if desired.

4. Transfer the hot mixture to the prepared sheet and let it spread into an even layer. Let cool for about 30 minutes until hardened.

5. Remove the candy sheet from the pan and dust it with powdered sugar. Break the candy into pieces. Store in an airtight container at room temperature for up to 1 month.

CHOCOLATE-DIPPED S'MORES MARSHMALLOW BONBONS

Makes about 40 pieces

PREP TIME: 20 minutes

CHILLING TIME: 30 minutes

EQIPMENT: Large rimmed baking sheet, skewer

Ingredients:

- 40 marshmallows
- 12 ounces semisweet chocolate, chopped
- 2 tablespoons coconut oil
- 1½ cups finely crushed graham cracker crumbs

Directions:

1. Cover a large rimmed baking sheet with parchment paper.

2. Arrange the marshmallows on the prepared baking sheet in a single layer and place in the freezer while you prepare the coatings.

3. In a medium microwave-safe bowl, combine the chocolate and coconut oil. Microwave at 50 percent power, in 30-second intervals, stirring in between, until the chocolate is completely melted and the mixture is smooth.

4. Place the graham cracker crumbs in a wide, shallow bowl for dipping.

5. Use a skewer or toothpick to spear one of the chilled marshmallows and dip it first in the chocolate mixture to coat well and then in the graham cracker crumbs. Once coated, slide the marshmallow off the skewer and back onto the parchment-covered sheet, using a fork, if needed, to slide it off the skewer without disturbing the coating.

6. Refrigerate for about 30 minutes until the chocolate is completely set.

DARK CHOCOLATE, CHERRY, AND HAZELNUT BARK

Serves 12

PREP TIME: 5 minutes

CHILLING TIME: 30 minutes

EQIPMENT: Rimmed baking sheet

Ingredients:

- 12 ounces semisweet chocolate, chopped, or 1 (12-ounce) bag semisweet chocolate chips
- 1 cup toasted hazelnuts, chopped
- ½ cup dried cherries

Directions:

1. Line a rimmed baking sheet with parchment paper.
2. Dump the chocolate into the prepared baking pan and spread it into an even layer. Place the pan in a cold oven and turn the heat to 350°F. Bake for 6 to 8 minutes, until the chocolate is soft and mostly melted.
3. Remove from the oven and use a knife or a rubber spatula to swirl and spread the chocolate around, which will help it melt completely.
4. While the chocolate is still warm and melty, sprinkle the chopped hazelnuts and dried cherries over the top. Refrigerate for about 30 minutes until set.
5. To serve, remove from the refrigerator and break it into pieces. Store leftovers in a covered container at room temperature.

S'MORES CHOCOLATE BARK

Serves 12

PREP TIME: 15 minutes

CHILLING TIME: 1 hour

EQIPMENT: 8-by-11-inch baking pan

Ingredients:

- 12 ounces milk chocolate, chopped, or 1 (12-ounce) bag milk chocolate chips
- 4 to 6 graham crackers, broken into small pieces
- 1 cup mini marshmallows
- ½ cup white chocolate chips
- 1 cup marshmallow cream

Directions:

1. Line an 8-by-11-inch baking pan with parchment paper.
2. Put the milk chocolate into the prepared pan and spread it into an even layer. Place the pan in a cold oven and turn the heat to 350°F. Bake for 6 to 8 minutes until the chocolate is soft and mostly melted.
3. Remove from the oven and use a knife or a rubber spatula to swirl and spread the chocolate around, which will help it melt completely.
4. While the chocolate is still warm and melty, sprinkle the graham cracker pieces and marshmallows over

the top. Refrigerate for about 30 minutes until set.

5. While the milk chocolate layer chills, in a medium microwave-safe bowl, microwave the white chocolate chips at 50 percent power, in 30-second intervals, stirring in between, until fully melted and smooth.

6. Add the marshmallow cream and microwave again at 50 percent power, in 30-second intervals, stirring in between, until the mixture is smooth. Immediately spread the marshmallow layer over the set chocolate layer. Refrigerate for about 30 minutes until completely set.

7. To serve, break the bark into pieces. Store refrigerated in a covered container.

ROCKY ROAD CHOCOLATE CRUNCH BARS

Serves 12

PREP TIME: 5 minutes

CHILLING TIME: 30 minutes

EQIPMENT: 8-inch square baking pan

Ingredients:

- 24 ounces milk chocolate, chopped, or 2 (12-ounce) bags milk chocolate chips
- 2½ cups crisped rice cereal
- 1 cup mini marshmallows

Directions:

1. Line an 8-inch square baking pan with parchment paper.

2. In a large microwave-safe bowl, microwave the chocolate at 50 percent power, in 30-second intervals, stirring in between, until fully melted and smooth.

3. Using a plastic spatula, gently fold the cereal and marshmallows into the chocolate. Transfer the mixture to the prepared pan and spread it into an even layer. Refrigerate for about 30 minutes until set.

4. Cut into bars and serve chilled or at room temperature.

PEANUT BUTTER FUDGE

Makes about 32 bars

PREP TIME: 10 minutes

CHILLING TIME: 3 hours

EQIPMENT: 8-inch square baking pan

Ingredients:

- Nonstick baking spray
- 2 cups sugar
- ½ cup low-fat or whole milk
- 1 cup peanut butter (smooth or crunchy)
- 1 teaspoon vanilla extract

Directions:

1. Coat an 8-inch square baking pan with nonstick baking spray.

2. In a medium saucepan set over medium-high heat, combine the sugar and milk. Bring to a boil. Let the

mixture boil for about 3 minutes, stirring frequently, and lowering the heat if necessary to keep it from boiling over the side. Remove the pan from the heat.

3. Stir in the peanut butter until it is completely melted and the mixture is smooth.

4. Stir in the vanilla. Transfer the peanut butter mixture to the prepared pan and let cool. Refrigerate for about 3 hours until completely set.

5. To serve, slice into 1-by-2-inch bars. Store in an airtight container at room temperature for up to 1 week, or refrigerate for up to 1 month.

WHITE AND DARK CHOCOLATE FUDGE

Makes about 32 bars

PREP TIME: 20 minutes
CHILLING TIME: 3 hours
EQIPMENT: 8-inch square baking pan

Ingredients:

- Nonstick baking spray
- 3 cups mini marshmallows
- 2 cups sugar
- 1 cup heavy (whipping) cream
- 6 tablespoons (¾ stick) unsalted butter
- Pinch salt
- 3 cups semisweet chocolate chips
- 1½ teaspoons vanilla extract
- ½ cup white chocolate chips

Directions:

1. Line an 8-inch square baking pan with parchment paper and generously coat the parchment with nonstick baking spray.

2. In a medium saucepan set over medium heat, combine the marshmallows, sugar, cream, butter, and salt. Cook for about 5 minutes, stirring frequently, until the butter and marshmallows are mostly melted. Raise the heat to medium-high and bring the mixture to a boil. Cook for 5 minutes more, stirring occasionally. Remove the pan from the heat.

3. Stir in the semisweet chocolate chips and the vanilla. Continue to stir until the chocolate is fully melted and the mixture is smooth. Pour the hot mixture into the prepared pan.

4. In a small microwave-safe bowl, microwave the white chocolate chips at 50 percent power, in 30-second intervals, stirring in between, until fully melted and smooth. Drizzle the melted white chocolate into the dark chocolate mixture. Using the tip of a knife, a chopstick, or a skewer, swirl the two together. Let cool to room temperature.

5. Once the fudge cools, refrigerate for about 3 hours until completely set. Slice into 1-by-2-inch bars and serve.

DARK CHOCOLATE TRUFFLES

Makes about 30 truffles

PREP TIME: 30 minutes

CHILLING TIME: 2 hours

EQIPMENT: Baking sheet

Ingredients:

- 12 ounces dark chocolate, chopped
- 3 tablespoons unsalted butter
- ⅓ cup heavy (whipping) cream
- 1 teaspoon vanilla extract
- Coatings as desired, such as sweetened or unsweetened cocoa powder, decorating sugars, colored sprinkles, finely chopped nuts, or shredded coconut

Directions:

1. In a large microwave-safe bowl, combine the dark chocolate, butter, and cream. Microwave at 50 percent power, in 30-second intervals, stirring in between, until the chocolate is fully melted and the mixture is smooth.
2. Whisk in the vanilla. Let the mixture cool to room temperature, cover with plastic wrap, and refrigerate for 2 hours.
3. Line the baking sheet with parchment paper.
4. With a small cookie scoop or a melon baller, scoop out balls of the chocolate. Gently roll the balls between your hands to smooth the edges. Place each ball on the prepared baking sheet once it is formed. Repeat until all the chocolate mixture has been used. You should get around 30 balls.
5. Place your desired coating(s) into shallow dishes and roll the balls in them to coat well. Return the coated balls to the baking sheet. Once all the balls are coated, refrigerate until ready to serve.

DARK CHOCOLATE SORBET

Serves 8

PREP TIME: 15 minutes

CHILLING AND FREEZING TIME: 5 to 6 hours

EQIPMENT: Freezer-safe storage container

Ingredients:

- 1 cup sugar
- ¾ cup unsweetened Dutch process cocoa powder
- Pinch salt
- 6 ounces semisweet chocolate, finely chopped
- 1 teaspoon vanilla extract

Directions:

1. In a large saucepan over medium-high heat, whisk the sugar, cocoa powder, salt, and 1¼ cups water. Bring to a boil and let it cook for about 45 seconds, whisking constantly. Remove from the heat and immediately add the chocolate. Stir until the chocolate completely melts and the mixture is smooth.
2. Stir in the vanilla and 1 cup water. Refrigerate for at least 2 hours until fully chilled.

3. Pour the mixture into a freezer-safe storage container, cover with plastic wrap, and freeze for about 45 minutes before checking on it the first time. As soon as it begins to freeze around the edges, mix it vigorously with a whisk, spatula, wooden spoon, or ideally, a handheld electric mixer or immersion blender. Continue to freeze, mixing it every 30 minutes, until it is fully frozen, 3 to 4 hours total.

4. Keep frozen until ready to serve.

LEMON SORBET

Serves 8

PREP TIME: 20 minutes

CHILLING AND FREEZING TIME: 5 to 6 hours

EQIPMENT: Freezer-safe storage container

Ingredients:

- 2 cups light corn syrup
- 1½ cups cold water
- 1 cup freshly squeezed lemon juice (from about 6 lemons)
- 1 tablespoon vodka
- Zest of 1 lemon
- ½ teaspoon salt

Directions:

1. In a medium bowl, whisk the corn syrup, water, lemon juice, vodka, lemon zest, and salt until smooth and well combined. Refrigerate for at least 2 hours until fully chilled.

2. Pour the mixture into a freezer-safe storage container, cover with plastic wrap, and freeze for about 45 minutes before checking on it the first time. As soon as it begins to freeze around the edges, mix it vigorously with a whisk, spatula, wooden spoon, or ideally, a handheld electric mixer or immersion blender. Continue to freeze, mixing it every 30 minutes, until it is fully frozen, 3 to 4 hours total.

3. Keep frozen until ready to serve.

TROPICAL ICE POPS

Makes 10 ice pops

PREP TIME: 5 minutes

FREEZING TIME: 6 hours

EQIPMENT: Blender, 10 ice pop molds or small paper cups and ice pop sticks

Ingredients:

- 4 cups frozen pineapple
- 1 cup canned coconut milk
- 2 teaspoons vanilla extract
- 2 tablespoons sugar, as needed

Directions:

1. In a blender, purée the pineapple, coconut milk, and vanilla until smooth. Taste and add sugar as needed, blending to incorporate it.

2. Pour the mixture into 10 ice pop molds or paper cups and freeze for about 45 minutes before adding the sticks. Freeze for at least 6 hours until frozen solid. Keep frozen.

WATERMELON ICE POPS

Makes 10 ice pops

PREP TIME: 20 minutes

FREEZING TIME: 7 hours

EQIPMENT: Blender, 10 ice pop molds or small paper cups and ice pop sticks

Ingredients:

- 3½ cups cubed seedless watermelon
- 5 tablespoons sugar, divided
- 1 tablespoon freshly squeezed lemon juice
- 1 tablespoon mini chocolate chips
- 10 kiwi fruits, peeled and diced

Directions:

1. In a blender, combine the watermelon with 2 tablespoons of sugar and the lemon juice and blend until smooth. Pour the mixture into 10 ice pop molds, filling the molds two-thirds full.
2. Add a few chocolate chips to each mold, pressing them down into the juice with one of the ice pop sticks or a skewer. Freeze for at least 4 hours.
3. Meanwhile, in a blender, combine the kiwi with the remaining 3 tablespoons of sugar and blend until smooth. Strain the mixture through a fine-mesh sieve to remove the seeds. Chill for at least 30 minutes.
4. Once the watermelon layer is frozen, remove the molds from the freezer and top off each mold with 2 tablespoons of kiwi mixture and insert the sticks. Return to the freezer and freeze for at least 3 hours more until solid.

ESPRESSO FROZEN YOGURT POPS

Makes 10 frozen yogurt pops

PREP TIME: 5 minutes

FREEZING TIME: 6 hours, 45 minutes

EQIPMENT: 10 ice pop molds or small paper cups and ice pop sticks

Ingredients:

- 3 cups vanilla yogurt
- ⅔ cup low-fat or whole milk
- ½ cup sugar
- 2 tablespoons instant espresso powder

Directions:

1. In a large pitcher, stir together the yogurt, milk, sugar, and espresso powder until well combined. Pour the mixture into 10 ice pop molds.
2. Freeze for at least 45 minutes before inserting the sticks. Freeze for at least 6 hours until frozen solid. Keep frozen until ready to serve

ROCKY ROAD CHOCOLATE CRUNCH BARS

Serves 12

PREP TIME: 5 minutes

CHILLING TIME: 30 minutes

EQIPMENT: 8-inch square baking pan

Ingredients:

- 24 ounces milk chocolate, chopped, or 2 (12-ounce) bags milk chocolate chips
- 2½ cups crisped rice cereal
- 1 cup mini marshmallows

Directions:

5. Line an 8-inch square baking pan with parchment paper.
6. In a large microwave-safe bowl, microwave the chocolate at 50 percent power, in 30-second intervals, stirring in between, until fully melted and smooth.
7. Using a plastic spatula, gently fold the cereal and marshmallows into the chocolate. Transfer the mixture to the prepared pan and spread it into an even layer. Refrigerate for about 30 minutes until set.
8. Cut into bars and serve chilled or at room temperature.

PEANUT BUTTER FUDGE

Makes about 32 bars

PREP TIME: 10 minutes

CHILLING TIME: 3 hours

EQIPMENT: 8-inch square baking pan

Ingredients:

- Nonstick baking spray
- 2 cups sugar
- ½ cup low-fat or whole milk
- 1 cup peanut butter (smooth or crunchy)
- 1 teaspoon vanilla extract

Directions:

6. Coat an 8-inch square baking pan with nonstick baking spray.
7. In a medium saucepan set over medium-high heat, combine the sugar and milk. Bring to a boil. Let the mixture boil for about 3 minutes, stirring frequently, and lowering the heat if necessary to keep it from boiling over the side. Remove the pan from the heat.
8. Stir in the peanut butter until it is completely melted and the mixture is smooth.
9. Stir in the vanilla. Transfer the peanut butter mixture to the prepared pan and let cool. Refrigerate for about 3 hours until completely set.
10. To serve, slice into 1-by-2-inch bars. Store in an airtight container at room temperature for up to 1 week, or refrigerate for up to 1 month.

WHITE AND DARK CHOCOLATE FUDGE

Makes about 32 bars

PREP TIME: 20 minutes

CHILLING TIME: 3 hours

EQIPMENT: 8-inch square baking pan

Ingredients:

- Nonstick baking spray
- 3 cups mini marshmallows
- 2 cups sugar
- 1 cup heavy (whipping) cream
- 6 tablespoons (¾ stick) unsalted butter
- Pinch salt
- 3 cups semisweet chocolate chips
- 1½ teaspoons vanilla extract
- ½ cup white chocolate chips

Directions:

6. Line an 8-inch square baking pan with parchment paper and generously coat the parchment with nonstick baking spray.

7. In a medium saucepan set over medium heat, combine the marshmallows, sugar, cream, butter, and salt. Cook for about 5 minutes, stirring frequently, until the butter and marshmallows are mostly melted. Raise the heat to medium-high and bring the mixture to a boil. Cook for 5 minutes more, stirring occasionally. Remove the pan from the heat.

8. Stir in the semisweet chocolate chips and the vanilla. Continue to stir until the chocolate is fully melted and the mixture is smooth. Pour the hot mixture into the prepared pan.

9. In a small microwave-safe bowl, microwave the white chocolate chips at 50 percent power, in 30-second intervals, stirring in between, until fully melted and smooth. Drizzle the melted white chocolate into the dark chocolate mixture. Using the tip of a knife, a chopstick, or a skewer, swirl the two together. Let cool to room temperature.

10. Once the fudge cools, refrigerate for about 3 hours until completely set. Slice into 1-by-2-inch bars and serve.

MIMOSA JELLY CANDIES

Makes 64 (1-inch) candies

PREP TIME: 5 minutes

COOK TIME: 30 minutes

CHILLING AND SETTING TIME: 28 to 52 hours

EQIPMENT: 8-inch square baking pan

Ingredients:

- Nonstick baking spray

- 3 tablespoons unflavored gelatin (about 4 envelopes)
- 3 cups sugar, plus more for coating the candies
- ¼ to ½ teaspoon orange flavoring oil
- ¼ to ½ teaspoon champagne flavoring oil
- Orange food coloring, for coloring the candies

Directions:

1. Line an 8-inch square baking pan with plastic wrap (let the plastic wrap hang over the sides of the pan for easy removal) and spray with nonstick baking spray.
2. Put ¾ cup cold water into a medium saucepan, sprinkle the gelatin evenly over the top, and let sit for 5 minutes.
3. In another pot or a kettle, bring 1 cup plus 2 tablespoons water to a boil. Once the gelatin has been sitting in the cold water for 5 minutes, add the boiling water to the saucepan. Stir the mixture until the gelatin dissolves completely.
4. Add the sugar and stir to combine. Place the saucepan over medium-high heat and bring the mixture to a boil. Lower the heat to medium and simmer for 25 minutes, stirring constantly. Remove the pan from the heat.
5. Stir in the orange and champagne flavoring oils to taste. Add orange food coloring to your desired color. Pour the hot mixture into the prepared pan. Cover with plastic wrap and refrigerate for at least 4 hours until completely set.
6. Lift the set jelly from the pan using the plastic wrap. Peel off the plastic and dredge the whole jelly in sugar, coating it evenly. Using a sharp knife sprayed with nonstick baking spray, cut the jelly into small squares (½ inch to 1 inch). Roll the cut candies in the sugar to coat the cut edges and place them in a single layer on parchment paper.
7. Let sit, uncovered, at room temperature for 24 to 48 hours, until the sugar crystalizes. Store in an airtight container at room temperature for up to 3 weeks.

BLACKBERRY FROZEN YOGURT SWIRL POPS

Makes 10 frozen yogurt pops

PREP TIME: 10 minutes
COOK TIME: 10 minutes
CHILLING AND FREEZING TIME: 6 hours, 30 minutes
EQIPMENT: Medium saucepan, blender, 10 ice pop molds or small paper cups and ice pop sticks

Ingredients:

- 2 cups fresh blackberries, halved if large
- 1 tablespoon freshly squeezed lemon juice
- ½ cup plus 2 tablespoons sugar, divided
- 1½ cups plain yogurt

Directions:

1. In a medium bowl, toss the berries with the lemon juice and 2 tablespoons of sugar. Set aside.
2. In a medium saucepan set over medium-high heat, combine ½ cup water with the remaining ½ cup of sugar and cook, stirring, until the water boils and the sugar dissolves. Lower the heat and simmer for 5

minutes more until the mixture is syrupy. Remove from the heat and transfer to a storage container or pitcher. Refrigerate for about 30 minutes until chilled.

3. In another medium bowl, whisk the yogurt with the chilled syrup.

4. In a blender, purée the berries until mostly smooth. Strain through a fine-mesh sieve into a bowl to remove the seeds.

5. To make the ice pops, fill the molds with alternating layers of yogurt mixture and berry purée until the molds are full. Leave about ½ inch at the top to allow for expansion as they freeze. Use an ice pop stick, skewer, or chopstick to gently swirl together the two mixtures. Transfer the pops to the freezer for about 45 minutes before inserting the sticks. Continue to freeze for at least 6 hours until frozen. Keep frozen until ready to serve.

WITH CHOCOLATE COOKIES

Makes 12 ice cream sandwiches

PREP TIME: 30 minutes

COOK TIME: 10 to 12 minutes

CHILLING AND FREEZING TIME: 1 hour, 30 minutes

EQIPMENT: 9-by-13-inch baking pan, electric mixer

Ingredients:

- ½ gallon vanilla ice cream, slightly softened
- 2 ⅔ cups all-purpose flour, plus more for the work surface
- ⅔ cup plus ¼ cup unsweetened cocoa powder
- ¾ teaspoon salt
- 1¼ cups (2½ sticks) unsalted butter
- 1 cup sugar
- 2 egg yolks
- 2 teaspoons vanilla extract

Directions:

1. Line a 9-by-13-inch baking pan with parchment paper (use enough paper so it hangs over the sides). Transfer the softened ice cream to the prepared pan and use a rubber spatula to spread it into an even layer. Cover with plastic wrap and freeze for at least 1 hour until frozen solid.

2. Preheat the oven to 350°F.

3. Line 2 baking sheets with parchment paper.

4. Meanwhile, in a medium bowl sift together the flour, cocoa powder, and salt.

5. In a large bowl, using a handheld electric mixer or a stand mixer at medium speed, cream together the butter and sugar for about 1 minute until creamy and lightened in color.

6. Add the egg yolks and vanilla and mix to incorporate.

7. Add the dry ingredients and mix until just combined. Split the dough into 2 equal pieces and pat each piece into a 5-inch square. Wrap the squares in plastic wrap and refrigerate for 30 minutes.

8. When the dough is thoroughly chilled, turn it out onto a lightly floured surface and roll each square into an 8-by-12-inch rectangle. Cut each rectangle into 6 (2-by-8-inch) strips. Halve each strip widthwise to make 24 (2-by-4-inch) rectangles. Transfer the cookies to the prepared sheets, and using a skewer or chopstick, make 2 lines of holes running down the length of each cookie. Bake for 10 to 12 minutes until firm.

9. Remove from the oven and transfer the cookies to a wire rack to cool completely.

10. When the cookies are completely cooled, lift the ice cream out of the baking pan using the parchment paper. Trim the edges so they are straight, creating a straight-sided 8-by-12-inch rectangle. Cut the ice cream into 6 (2-by-8-inch) strips and halve each strip widthwise to make 12 (2-by-4-inch) rectangles.

11. Place each ice cream rectangle between 2 cookies and press together slightly. Serve immediately or wrap in parchment paper or plastic wrap and freeze.

CHOCOLATE-HAZELNUT FUDGE POPS

Makes 6 ice pops

PREP TIME: 10 minutes

FREEZING TIME: 6 hours

EQIPMENT: Medium saucepan, 6 ice pop molds or small paper cups and ice pop sticks

Ingredients:

- 1 cup whole milk
- 1 cup chocolate-hazelnut spread (like Nutella)
- ½ cup heavy (whipping) cream
- 2 tablespoons dark cocoa powder
- 1 teaspoon vanilla extract

Directions:

1. In a medium saucepan set over low heat, stir together the milk, chocolate-hazelnut spread, cream, cocoa powder, and vanilla for 5 to 10 minutes until the chocolate-hazelnut spread is fully melted and the mixture is well combined. Remove from the heat and set aside to cool for about 10 minutes.

2. Pour the chocolate mixture into 6 ice pop molds or paper cups set on a sheet pan. Freeze for about 45 minutes before adding the sticks. Continue to freeze for at least 6 hours until completely frozen solid. Keep frozen until ready to serve.

TIRAMISU ICE CREAM CAKE

Serves 8

PREP TIME: 30 minutes

FREEZING TIME: 6 hours, 30 minutes

EQIPMENT: 9-inch springform pan

Ingredients:

- Nonstick baking spray, for preparing the pan
- 25 chocolate wafer cookies, finely crushed, plus more for garnish (I prefer Nabisco Famous Chocolate Wafers)
- 2 tablespoons unsalted butter, melted
- 3 pints coffee ice cream, divided
- 1½ cups brewed espresso or strong coffee, cooled
- 30 soft ladyfingers, divided
- 1 cup heavy (whipping) cream
- 2 tablespoons sugar

- ¼ cup finely grated semisweet chocolate, or cocoa powder

Directions:

1. Coat the inside of a 9-inch springform pan with nonstick baking spray.

2. In a small bowl, stir together the cookie crumbs and butter. Press the mixture into the bottom of the prepared pan. Transfer the pan to the freezer.

3. Let the ice cream sit on the countertop at room temperature for about 15 minutes until it softens. Transfer to a large bowl and stir it until it softens into a spreadable consistency.

4. Remove the pan from the freezer and spread ⅓ of the ice cream over the crust. Dip the ladyfingers into the coffee and arrange them in a single layer covering the layer of ice cream. Repeat twice more so you have 3 layers of ice cream separated by 3 layers of espresso-dipped ladyfingers. Cover with plastic wrap and return to the freezer for about 30 minutes.

5. In a large bowl, combine the cream and sugar, using a handheld electric mixer or a stand mixer to whip the ingredients until the cream holds soft peaks.

6. Remove the pan from the freezer again and spread the whipped cream over the top. Garnish with the shaved chocolate or cocoa powder, cover with plastic wrap, and return the pan to the freezer for at least 6 hours.

7. To serve, unmold the cake from the springform pan and slice it into wedges. Serve straight out of the freezer and keep any unused portion covered and frozen.

STRAWBERRY SHORTCAKE

Serves 6

PREP TIME: 20 minutes

COOK TIME: 18 to 20 minutes

CHILLING AND COOLING TIME: 45 minutes

EQIPMENT: 8-inch square baking pan, electric mixer

Ingredients:

- 1½ pounds fresh strawberries, stemmed and quartered
- ½ cup sugar, divided
- 2 cups all-purpose flour
- 2 teaspoons baking powder
- ¾ teaspoon salt
- ¼ teaspoon baking soda
- 3 cups chilled heavy (whipping) cream, divided
- 1½ teaspoons vanilla extract

Directions:

1. In a large bowl, toss the strawberries with 3 tablespoons of sugar. Refrigerate for at least 30 minutes to let the strawberries macerate.

2. Preheat the oven to 400°F.

3. In a medium bowl, stir together the flour, baking powder, baking soda, salt, and 2 tablespoons of sugar.

4. Add 1½ cups of cream and stir until just combined. Transfer the batter to an 8-inch square baking pan and bake for 18 to 20 minutes until golden brown.

5. Remove from the oven and invert the cake onto a wire rack to cool.

6. While the cake cools, make the whipped cream. Using a handheld electric mixer or a stand mixer, beat the remaining 1½ cups of cream with the remaining 3 tablespoons of sugar for about 3 minutes until the cream holds soft peaks.

7. Add the vanilla and beat to incorporate.

8. Once cooled, cut the cake into 6 rectangular pieces and split each horizontally. Put the bottom halves of the cake onto 6 serving plates and spoon some of the strawberries, along with the juice that has collected in the bowl, over them. Add a generous dollop of whipped cream and top with the cake tops. Serve immediately.

ESPRESSO ICEBOX CAKE

Serves 8

PREP TIME: 20 minutes

CHILLING AND FREEZING TIME: 9 hours

EQIPMENT: 10-inch springform pan, electric mixer

Ingredients:

- 3 cups chilled heavy (whipping) cream, divided
- ½ cup plus 1 tablespoon sugar, divided
- 1 cup (about 9 ounces) mascarpone cheese, at room temperature
- ¼ cup coffee liqueur, such as Kahlua
- 42 chocolate wafer cookies, divided (I prefer Nabisco Famous Chocolate Wafers)
- 1 tablespoon instant espresso powder

Directions:

1. In a large bowl, using a handheld electric mixer or in a stand mixer, beat together 2 cups of cream with 6 tablespoons of sugar for about 3 minutes until the cream holds soft peaks.

2. With the mixer set on low speed, add the mascarpone and coffee liqueur. Mix to combine.

3. Spread 1¼ cups of the mascarpone mixture over the bottom of the springform pan in an even layer. Top with 14 chocolate wafers, slightly overlapping them as needed. Top the wafers with another 1¼ cups of mascarpone and another layer of 14 wafers. Top with the remaining mascarpone, smoothing the top with a spatula. Cover the pan and freeze for about 1 hour until the cake is firm. Transfer the cake to the refrigerator and chill for 8 hours or longer until the cookies are soft and the cake is set.

4. Crush the remaining wafers in a blender, food processor, or in a resealable plastic bag with a rolling pin.

5. In a medium bowl, using an electric mixer or a stand mixer set at medium speed, whip the remaining 1 cup of cream with the espresso powder and the remaining 3 tablespoons of sugar for about 3 minutes, just until the cream holds stiff peaks.

6. Unmold the cake from the pan, spread the espresso cream over the top and sides, and sprinkle the wafer crumbs over the top. Serve chilled.

WHITE CHOCOLATE–RASPBERRY SWIRL CHEESECAKE

Serves 10

PREP TIME: 20 minutes

COOK TIME: 35 to 40 minutes

CHILLING TIME: 3 hours

EQIPMENT: Electric mixer, 9-inch springform pan

Ingredients:

- 2 cups chocolate wafer cookie crumbs (I prefer Nabisco Famous Chocolate Wafers)
- 4 tablespoons (½ stick) unsalted butter, melted
- 2 (8-ounce) packages cream cheese, at room temperature
- ½ cup sugar
- ½ teaspoon vanilla extract
- 2 eggs
- 3 ounces white chocolate, melted
- 3 tablespoons raspberry preserves

Directions:

1. Preheat the oven to 350°F.
2. In a small bowl, combine the cookie crumbs and melted butter. Press the mixture into the bottom and partway up the sides of a 9-inch springform pan.
3. In a medium bowl, using a handheld electric mixer or in a stand mixer, beat together the cream cheese, sugar, and vanilla.
4. Add the eggs and beat until just combined.
5. Stir in the white chocolate and pour the batter into the prepared crust.
6. Put the preserves in a small microwave-safe bowl and microwave at high power for about 20 seconds to melt. Using a small spoon, dollop the preserves on top of the cheesecake. Use the tip of a knife to drag and swirl the preserves through the batter. Bake for 35 to 40 minutes until the center is mostly set.
7. Remove from the oven and let cool. Refrigerate for at least 3 hours before serving.

BLACKBERRY CRUMB CAKE

Serves 8

PREP TIME: 10 minutes

COOK TIME: 45 minutes

EQIPMENT: Electric mixer, 8-inch square or round cake pan

Ingredients:

FOR THE TOPPING

- ½ cup old-fashioned rolled oats
- ½ cup packed brown sugar
- ¼ cup all-purpose flour
- 4 tablespoons (½ stick) cold unsalted butter

FOR THE CAKE

- 4 tablespoons (½ stick) unsalted butter, at room temperature, plus more for preparing the baking pan
- 1¾ cups all-purpose flour, plus more for preparing the baking pan
- ¾ cup sugar
- 1 egg
- 1 teaspoon vanilla extract

- Zest of 1 lemon
- 2 teaspoons baking powder
- ½ teaspoon salt
- ½ cup low-fat or whole milk
- 2 heaping cups fresh blackberries, halved if large

Directions:

TO MAKE THE TOPPING

1. In a medium bowl, stir together the oats, brown sugar, and flour. Using your fingers, mix in the butter until it is incorporated and the mixture forms coarse crumbs.

TO MAKE THE CAKE

1. Preheat the oven to 375°F.
2. Butter and flour an 8-inch cake pan. Line the pan with parchment paper, using enough that it hangs over the sides (to make cake removal easier).
3. In a large bowl, using a handheld electric mixer or a stand mixer, cream together the butter and sugar until fluffy and light.
4. Add the egg, vanilla, and lemon zest and mix to incorporate.
5. In a medium bowl, combine the flour, baking powder, and salt.
6. Add the dry ingredients and the milk to the wet ingredients in 3 alternating batches (one-third of the dry mixture followed by one-third of the milk), stirring in between to incorporate.
7. Fold in the blackberries. Transfer the batter to the prepared pan and sprinkle the topping evenly over the batter. Bake for about 45 minutes until a toothpick inserted into the center comes out clean.
8. Remove from the oven and let the cake cool in the pan. Lift the cake out of the pan, cut it into squares or wedges, and serve.

PEACH UPSIDE-DOWN CAKE

Serves 8

PREP TIME: 15 minutes

COOK TIME: 45 to 50 minutes

EQIPMENT: 9-inch round cake pan

Ingredients:

- Unsalted butter, for preparing the pan

FOR THE TOPPING

- ½ cup packed brown sugar
- 4 tablespoons (½ stick) unsalted butter, melted
- 5 peaches, peeled and cut into ¼-inch thick slices

FOR THE CAKE

- 1 ⅓ cups all-purpose flour
- 1½ teaspoons baking powder
- ¼ teaspoon salt
- ½ cup (1 stick) unsalted butter, at room temperature
- ⅓ cup granulated sugar

- ⅓ cup packed brown sugar
- 1 egg
- ¼ cup low-fat or whole milk
- 2 teaspoons vanilla extract

Directions:

1. Grease the bottom and sides of a 9-inch round cake pan with butter.

TO MAKE THE TOPPING

1. In a small bowl, mix together the brown sugar and melted butter. Spread it into the bottom of the prepared pan.
2. Starting from the middle of the pan, arrange the peach slices, covering the entire surface and layering the fruit as needed.

TO MAKE THE CAKE

1. Preheat the oven to 350°F.
2. In a small bowl, stir together the flour, baking powder, and salt.
3. In a medium bowl, with a handheld electric mixer, a stand mixer, or a wooden spoon, cream together the butter, granulated sugar, and brown sugar.
4. Add the egg, milk, and vanilla. Beat to mix well.
5. Add the dry ingredients and beat on low speed until fully incorporated. Spoon the batter evenly over the peaches and carefully smooth it into an even layer. Bake for 45 to 50 minutes until golden brown and springy to the touch.
6. Remove from the oven and let the cake cool in the pan for 5 minutes. To unmold the cake, run a sharp knife around the edge of the pan and place an inverted serving platter on top. Carefully invert the cake so it falls out onto the platter. Slice into wedges and serve.

PINEAPPLE UPSIDE-DOWN CUPCAKES

Makes 12 cupcakes

PREP TIME: 15 minutes

COOK TIME: 24 to 26 minutes

EQIPMENT: 12-cup muffin tin, electric mixer

Ingredients:

- Nonstick baking spray
- 1 (20-ounce) can and 1 (8-ounce) can pineapple chunks in juice, drained with ½ cup juice reserved
- ⅓ cup packed brown sugar
- ⅓ cup unsalted butter, melted, plus 4 tablespoons (½ stick), at room temperature
- 1 cup all-purpose flour
- ¾ cup plus 2 tablespoons granulated sugar, divided
- ½ teaspoon baking powder
- ¼ teaspoon salt
- 1 egg
- ½ teaspoon vanilla extract
- ¾ cup heavy (whipping) cream

- 12 maraschino cherries

Directions:

1. Preheat the oven to 350°F.
2. Spray a 12-cup muffin tin with nonstick baking spray.
3. Place several layers of paper towels on a plate and spread the drained pineapple chunks on top to drain thoroughly.
4. In a small bowl, stir together the brown sugar and melted butter. Spoon the mixture into the muffin cups, coating the bottom of each with about 2 teaspoons of the mixture.
5. Arrange about 5 pineapple chunks in a single layer in the bottom of each muffin cup.
6. In a large bowl, using a handheld electric mixer or a stand mixer, combine the flour, ¾ cup of granulated sugar, the baking powder, and salt.
7. Add the room temperature butter and the reserved ½ cup of pineapple juice and beat for 1 to 2 minutes.
8. Add the egg and vanilla and beat until just incorporated. Scoop the batter into the muffin cups over the pineapple chunks, filling each cup ¾ of the way full. Bake for 24 to 26 minutes, or until a toothpick inserted into the center of one of the cupcakes comes out clean.
9. Remove from the oven and let the cupcakes cool in the tin for about 5 minutes. To remove the cupcakes, run a sharp knife around the edge of each cup to loosen the cupcakes, and place a wire rack on top of the muffin tin and carefully invert it. The cupcakes should fall out onto the rack. Let the cupcakes cool completely on the rack before topping them.
10. While the cupcakes cool, in a large bowl, using an electric mixer with a whisk attachment or by hand using a whisk, whip the cream and remaining 2 tablespoons of granulated sugar until the cream holds stiff peaks. Dollop or pipe the whipped cream onto the cupcakes and top each with a maraschino cherry.

WITH COCONUT BUTTERCREAM FROSTING

Makes 12 cupcakes

PREP TIME: 20 minutes
COOK TIME: 18 to 20 minutes
EQIPMENT: 12-cup muffin tin, paper cupcake liners, electric mixer
Ingredients:
FOR THE CUPCAKES

- 1 cup all-purpose flour
- 1¼ teaspoons baking powder
- ¼ teaspoon salt
- ½ cup (1 stick) unsalted butter, at room temperature
- ¾ cup sugar
- 1 egg, at room temperature
- 1 egg white, at room temperature
- 1 teaspoon vanilla extract
- 1 teaspoon coconut extract
- ½ cup full-fat canned coconut milk

FOR THE FROSTING

- ¾ cup unsalted butter, kept at room temperature for 25 to 30 minutes before using
- 6 tablespoons full-fat canned coconut milk
- 2½ to 3 cups powdered sugar
- 1 teaspoon coconut extract
- 1 cup sweetened shredded coconut

Directions:

TO MAKE THE CUPCAKES

1. Preheat the oven to 350°F.
2. Line a 12-cup muffin tin with paper liners.
3. In a medium bowl, combine the flour, baking powder, and salt.
4. In a large bowl, using a handheld electric mixer or a stand mixer set on medium speed, cream together the butter and sugar for about 3 minutes until fluffy and pale.
5. Add the egg, egg white, and vanilla. Mix well to combine.
6. With the mixer on low speed, add the dry ingredients, coconut extract, and coconut milk in alternating batches, beating well after each addition. Scoop the batter into the prepared muffin tin, dividing equally. Bake for 18 to 20 minutes until a toothpick inserted into the center of one of the cupcakes comes out clean.
7. Remove from the oven and let the cupcakes cool in the pan for 10 minutes before removing them from the tin to a wire rack to cool completely.

TO MAKE THE FROSTING

1. In a large bowl, using a handheld electric mixer or a stand mixer, beat together the butter and coconut milk until creamy.
2. Add 2½ cups of powdered sugar and beat on medium-low speed until combined. Raise the speed to medium-high and continue to beat until the mixture is fluffy and light.
3. Add the coconut extract and more powdered sugar as needed to get a thick, spreadable consistency.
4. Once the cupcakes are completely cool, pipe or spread the frosting on top and sprinkle with the shredded coconut. Serve at room temperature.

CINNAMON CUSTARD

Serves 4

PREP TIME: 5 minutes

COOK TIME: 10 minutes

EQIPMENT: Medium saucepan, fine-mesh sieve

Ingredients:

- ½ cup sugar
- 2 (3-inch) cinnamon sticks, broken
- 1 cup low-fat or whole milk
- 1 cup heavy (whipping) cream
- 6 egg yolks, at room temperature
- 1 tablespoon cornstarch

- Ground cinnamon, for garnish

Directions:

1. Spread the sugar over the bottom of a medium saucepan set over medium heat. Add the cinnamon sticks and cook for about 5 minutes just until the sugar melts and turns golden.

2. Carefully pour in the milk and cream, being careful not to splatter, and bring the mixture to a boil.

3. In a large bowl, whisk the egg yolks and cornstarch. While whisking continuously, slowly add the hot milk mixture to the yolks. Return the mixture to the saucepan and place it over medium heat. Cook for about 5 minutes, stirring, until it thickens.

4. Strain the thickened mixture through a fine-mesh sieve into a serving bowl, discarding the cinnamon sticks. Garnish with a bit of ground cinnamon and serve warm. Cover any leftovers with plastic wrap and refrigerate for up to 3 days.

PLUM CUSTARD

Serves 6

PREP TIME: 10 minutes

COOK TIME: 45 minutes to 1 hour

EQIPMENT: 9-inch pie dish, fine-mesh sieve

Ingredients:

- Unsalted butter, for preparing the pan
- 1¼ cups low-fat or whole milk
- ⅓ cup sugar
- 2 eggs
- ½ cup all-purpose flour
- 1 tablespoon vanilla extract
- ⅛ teaspoon salt
- 4 plums, pitted and quartered
- Powdered sugar, for garnish

Directions:

1. Preheat the oven to 350°F.

2. Generously grease a 9-inch pie dish with butter.

3. In a medium bowl, whisk the milk, sugar, eggs, flour, vanilla, and salt. Strain the mixture through a fine-mesh sieve into the prepared pie dish.

4. Arrange the plum wedges on top of the batter.

5. Bake for 45 minutes to 1 hour until the cake is puffed, golden brown, and a toothpick inserted into the center comes out clean.

6. Garnish with powdered sugar, slice, and serve warm or at room temperature. Cover any leftovers with plastic wrap and refrigerate for up to 3 days.

ARBORIO RICE PUDDING

Serves 4 to 6

PREP TIME: 15 minutes (including 10 minutes to soak the rice)

COOK TIME: 1 hour

EQIPMENT: Medium saucepan, 8-inch square baking dish

Ingredients:

- 2 tablespoons unsalted butter, plus more for preparing the baking dish
- 1 cup uncooked arborio rice
- 2 cups whole milk
- ½ cup heavy (whipping) cream
- Pinch salt
- ¼ cup sugar
- 1 teaspoon vanilla extract
- ½ teaspoon ground cinnamon

Directions:

1. Preheat the oven to 325°F.
2. Generously grease an 8-inch square baking dish with butter.
3. In a medium saucepan, combine the rice, milk, cream, and salt. Let the rice soak for 10 minutes.
4. Place the saucepan over medium-high heat and bring just to a boil. Remove the saucepan from the heat and pour the rice mixture into the prepared dish.
5. Stir in the butter, sugar, and vanilla.
6. Sprinkle the cinnamon over the top. Bake for about 1 hour, until the rice is tender, all the liquid has been soaked up, and the top is golden brown.
7. Remove from the oven and serve warm. Cover any leftovers with plastic wrap and refrigerate for up to 3 days.

DARK CHOCOLATE PUDDING

Serves 4

PREP TIME: 5 minutes
COOK TIME: 4 minutes
EQIPMENT: Medium saucepan

Ingredients:

- ¼ cup cornstarch
- 3 tablespoons unsweetened cocoa powder
- ⅓ cup sugar
- ¼ teaspoon salt
- 3 cups whole milk
- 4 ounces dark chocolate, melted in the microwave (see tip)
- 2 teaspoons vanilla extract

Directions:

1. In a large saucepan, whisk the cornstarch, cocoa powder, sugar, and salt.
2. Add the milk and whisk until well combined. Place the saucepan over medium heat and bring to a simmer. Cook for about 4 minutes, whisking continuously, until the mixture thickens. Transfer the hot mixture to a medium bowl.
3. Whisk in the melted chocolate and vanilla. Serve immediately or cover with plastic wrap and refrigerate

for up to 3 days.

MANGO PUDDING

Serves 8

PREP TIME: 5 minutes
COOK TIME: 10 minutes
CHILLING TIME: 2 hours
EQIPMENT: 8 (6-ounce) ramekins, small saucepan, blender or food processor, fine-mesh sieve
Ingredients:

- 1¼ cups sugar, divided
- 2½ cups cold water, divided
- 1 pound frozen mango chunks
- 2 (¼-ounce) packets unflavored gelatin
- ½ teaspoon salt
- 1 cup heavy (whipping) cream, chilled
- 1 teaspoon freshly squeezed lime juice

Directions:

1. Arrange 8 (6-ounce) ramekins on a baking sheet.
2. In a small saucepan set over medium-high heat, combine ½ cup of sugar with ¾ cup of cold water and heat for about 4 minutes, stirring, until the sugar fully dissolves and the mixture comes to a boil.
3. In a blender or food processor, combine the frozen mango and sugar mixture. Process until smooth. Strain the mixture through a fine-mesh sieve into a medium bowl, discarding any solids.
4. In a small saucepan set over high heat, bring 1¼ cups water to a boil.
5. In a large bowl, whisk the remaining ¾ cup of sugar with the gelatin and salt.
6. Whisk in the remaining ½ cup of cold water and continue to whisk for about 30 seconds. Add the boiling water and continue to whisk for about 1 minute until the sugar and gelatin completely dissolve.
7. Stir in 2 cups of mango purée along with the heavy cream and lime juice, mixing until well combined. Spoon the mixture into the ramekins, dividing evenly. Refrigerate for at least 2 hours until firm. Serve chilled. Cover any leftovers with plastic wrap and refrigerate for up to 3 days.

LEMON PUDDING CAKE

Serves 6 to 8

PREP TIME: 15 minutes
COOK TIME: 45 minutes to 1 hour
EQIPMENT: 8-inch square or round cake pan, whisk, electric mixer
Ingredients:

- ½ cup (1 stick) unsalted butter, melted, plus more for preparing the baking dish
- 4 eggs, at room temperature, separated
- ¾ cup sugar
- 1 teaspoon vanilla extract
- ¾ cup all-purpose flour

- Zest of 1 lemon
- ¼ cup freshly squeezed lemon juice
- 1¾ cups low-fat or whole milk, slightly warmed
- Powdered sugar, for dusting

Directions:

1. Preheat the oven to 325°F.
2. Grease an 8-inch cake pan with butter.
3. In a large bowl, using an electric mixer, whip the egg whites until stiff peaks form.
4. In another large bowl, whisk the egg yolks and sugar until the mixture lightens.
5. Add the melted butter and vanilla and beat for 1 to 2 minutes more.
6. Add the flour and mix until it is fully incorporated.
7. Whisk in the lemon zest and juice.
8. While whisking or beating continuously, add the milk.
9. Gently fold in the egg whites, about ⅓ at a time, until they are mostly incorporated but bits of white are still visible. Transfer the batter to the prepared pan and bake for 45 minutes to 1 hour until the top is firm to the touch.
10. Remove from the oven and let the cake cool completely.
11. Dust the top with powdered sugar, and serve at room temperature. Cover any leftovers with plastic wrap and refrigerate for up to 3 days.

CHOCOLATE BROWNIE PUDDING CAKE

Serves 6 to 8

PREP TIME: 15 minutes
COOK TIME: 1 hour
EQIPMENT: 8-inch square or round cake pan, whisk, electric mixer

Ingredients:

- ½ cup (1 stick) unsalted butter, melted, plus more for preparing the pan
- ¼ cup plus 3 tablespoons all-purpose flour, plus more for preparing the pan
- 4 eggs, at room temperature, separated
- 1 tablespoon water
- 1 teaspoon vanilla extract
- Pinch salt
- ¼ cup plus 2 tablespoons unsweetened cocoa powder
- 2 cups low-fat or whole milk, slightly warmed
- 1 teaspoon vinegar
- ¾ cup powdered sugar

Directions:

1. Preheat the oven to 325°F.
2. Grease an 8-inch cake pan with butter and dust with flour.
3. In a large bowl, whisk the egg yolks with the water until the eggs become creamy and light.
4. Add the melted butter, vanilla, and salt and beat until the mixture is light and fluffy.

5. Add the flour and cocoa powder in 3 batches, mixing after each addition until thoroughly incorporated.

6. Add the milk, a little at a time, mixing thoroughly after each addition.

7. In another large bowl, with a handheld mixer or whisk, whip the egg whites and vinegar until stiff peaks form. Add a scoop of the whipped egg whites to the chocolate mixture and gently fold it in.

8. Add a scoop of the chocolate mixture to the egg whites and gently fold to combine. Continue adding the chocolate mixture a little at a time to the egg white mixture, gently folding it in. Transfer the batter to the prepared pan and bake for about 1 hour until the cake is mostly set, but still slightly jiggly in the center.

9. Remove from the oven and set the pan on a wire rack to cool completely before slicing and serving. Cover any leftovers with plastic wrap and refrigerate for up to 3 days.

VANILLA BEAN POTS DE CRÈME

Serves 8

PREP TIME: 15 minutes

COOK TIME: 25 to 30 minutes

CHILLING TIME: 4 hours

EQIPMENT: Medium saucepan, whisk, large baking dish, 8 (4-ounce) ramekins, fine-mesh sieve

Ingredients:

- 2 cups heavy (whipping) cream
- ½ cup whole milk
- ¼ teaspoon salt
- 1 vanilla bean, split lengthwise
- 6 egg yolks
- ¼ cup sugar
- Lightly sweetened whipped cream, for serving (optional)

Directions:

1. Preheat the oven to 300°F.

2. Place 8 (4-ounce) ramekins in a large baking dish.

3. In a medium saucepan set over medium heat, whisk the cream, milk, and salt.

4. Scrape the seeds from the inside of the vanilla bean into the cream, and then add the pod. Heat for about 4 minutes, stirring occasionally, until the mixture simmers.

5. Meanwhile, in a large bowl, whisk the egg yolks and sugar for about 4 minutes until the mixture becomes pale. While whisking continuously, add the hot cream mixture to the yolk mixture in a thin, slow stream. Continue whisking until the mixture is smooth. Strain it through a fine-mesh sieve into a large bowl or pitcher.

6. Ladle or pour the mixture into the ramekins, dividing evenly. Add enough hot water to the baking dish so it comes about halfway up the sides of the ramekins. Carefully transfer the baking dish to the oven and bake for 25 to 30 minutes until set around the edges, but still jiggly in the center.

7. Remove the baking dish from the oven and let the custards cool in the water bath for 5 minutes. Transfer the ramekins to a wire rack to cool completely. Refrigerate for at least 4 hours to chill. Serve chilled, topped with whipped cream (if using). Cover any leftovers with plastic wrap and refrigerate for up to 3 days.

ESPRESSO PANNA COTTA

Serves 4

PREP TIME: 15 minutes
COOK TIME: 5 minutes
CHILLING TIME: 4 hours
EQIPMENT: Small saucepan, 4 (6-ounce) ramekins
Ingredients:

- 1 cup whole milk
- 1 tablespoon unflavored powdered gelatin
- 3 cups heavy (whipping) cream
- ½ cup sugar
- 2 tablespoons instant espresso powder
- Pinch salt
- Dark chocolate shavings, for garnish (optional)

Directions:

1. In a small saucepan, add the milk and sprinkle the gelatin over it. Let sit for 5 minutes. Place the pan over medium heat and gently heat for about 2 minutes, stirring frequently, until the gelatin dissolves.
2. Stir in the cream, sugar, espresso powder, and salt. Turn the heat to low and continue to heat for about 3 minutes more, just until the sugar dissolves. Spoon the mixture into 4 (6-ounce) ramekins or custard cups, dividing equally. Cover and refrigerate, stirring once or twice during the first hour of chilling. Let chill for at least 4 hours.
3. Serve chilled, garnished with chocolate shavings (if using). Refrigerate any leftovers (see tip).

STRAWBERRY CLAFOUTIS

Serves 6

PREP TIME: 15 minutes
COOK TIME: 30 minutes
EQIPMENT: 9-inch round baking dish or pie dish, whisk
Ingredients:

- 3 tablespoons unsalted butter, melted, plus more for preparing the pan
- ½ cup all-purpose flour
- ¼ cup plus 2 tablespoons sugar
- Pinch salt
- 3 eggs
- Finely grated zest of 1 lemon
- ¼ cup plus 2 tablespoons low-fat or whole milk
- 3 cups halved or quartered fresh strawberries (about 1½ pints)
- Powdered sugar, for garnish

Directions:

1. Preheat the oven to 350°F.

2. Generously grease a 9-inch round baking dish or pie dish with butter.

3. In a large bowl, whisk the flour, sugar, and salt.

4. Add the eggs, melted butter, and lemon zest. Whisk until smooth.

5. Add the milk and continue whisking for about 3 minutes more until the mixture is smooth and light.

6. Arrange the strawberries in an even layer in the bottom of the prepared dish and pour the batter over the top. Bake for about 30 minutes until the top is golden and the center is set.

7. Remove from the oven and let cool for a few minutes. Dust with powdered sugar, slice into wedges, and serve immediately. Cover any leftovers with plastic wrap and refrigerate for up to 3 days.

KEY LIME MOUSSE PIE CUPS

Serves 10

PREP TIME: 15 minutes

CHILLING TIME: 1 hour

EQIPMENT: 10 (4-ounce) ramekins or custard cups, electric mixer

Ingredients:

- ⅔ cup graham cracker crumbs
- 2 teaspoons sugar
- 2 tablespoons unsalted butter, melted
- 2 cups cold heavy (whipping) cream
- 1 (14-ounce) can sweetened condensed milk
- ½ cup freshly squeezed key lime juice (from about 14 key limes)
- Lime zest (optional)

Directions:

1. In a small bowl, combine the graham cracker crumbs, sugar, and melted butter. Stir to mix well. Divide the mixture equally among 10 (4-ounce) ramekins or custard cups.

2. In a large bowl, using an electric mixer, whip the cream until stiff peaks form.

3. In another small bowl, whisk the sweetened condensed milk and lime juice. Gently fold the lime juice mixture into the whipped cream until incorporated. Spoon the mixture into the ramekins or custard cups on top of the graham cracker crust. Chill thoroughly, for at least 1 hour, and serve cold, garnished with the lime zest, if desired. Cover any leftovers with plastic wrap and refrigerate for up to 3 days.

CHOCOLATE MOUSSE

Serves 8

PREP TIME: 15 minutes

CHILLING TIME: 4 hours

EQIPMENT: Small saucepan, electric mixer with whisk attachment

Ingredients:

- 2 eggs
- ¼ cup sugar
- 2½ cups cold heavy (whipping) cream, divided

- 6 ounces semisweet chocolate, chopped

Directions:

1. In a large bowl, using an electric mixer, beat together the eggs and sugar for 3 minutes.

2. In a small saucepan set over medium heat, bring 1 cup of cream to a simmer. Do not let it boil.

3. With the mixer running, add the hot cream to the egg mixture in a slow, steady stream until it is thoroughly incorporated. Transfer the egg and cream mixture to the saucepan and place it over low heat. Cook for about 5 minutes, stirring constantly, until the mixture thickens.

4. Remove the pan from the heat and add the chocolate. Stir until the chocolate is completely melted and incorporated. Refrigerate, covered, for at least 2 hours, stirring occasionally.

5. When the mixture is fully chilled, use an electric mixer with a whisk attachment to whip the remaining 1½ cups of cream until stiff peaks form. Add the whipped cream to the chilled chocolate mixture, gently folding, until it is fully incorporated and the mixture is smooth.

6. Cover with plastic wrap and refrigerate for at least 2 hours to chill. Serve chilled. Cover any leftovers with plastic wrap and refrigerate for up to 3 days.

PEACHES AND CREAM

Serves 4

PREP TIME: 10 minutes

CHILLING TIME: 2 hours

EQIPMENT: Blender or food processor, 4 (8-ounce) ramekins, custard cups, or wineglasses

Ingredients:

- 3 tablespoons cold water
- 2¼ teaspoons (1 envelope) unflavored gelatin
- 5 cups diced peaches, divided
- ½ cup plus 2 teaspoons sugar, divided
- 1 teaspoon vanilla extract
- ¾ cup sour cream

Directions:

1. In a small microwave-safe bowl, stir together the water and gelatin. Microwave on high power for 20 seconds and stir. If the gelatin is not fully dissolved, return to the microwave for another 10 seconds on high power.

2. In a blender or food processor, combine 4 cups of peaches with ½ cup of the sugar and the vanilla. Process until smooth.

3. Add the sour cream and pulse to incorporate.

4. With the motor running on low, add the gelatin mixture in a slow steady stream. Divide the mixture evenly between 4 (8-ounce) ramekins, custard cups, or wineglasses, cover, and refrigerate for at least 2 hours, until set.

5. Before serving, in a small bowl, toss together the remaining 1 cup of diced peaches with the remaining 2 teaspoons of sugar and let macerate for about 2 minutes. Top each serving with some of the diced peaches and serve immediately. Cover any leftovers with plastic wrap and refrigerate for up to 3 days.

RASPBERRY PIE SQUARES

Makes 16 squares

PREP TIME: 20 minutes

COOKING TIME: 10 minutes

CHILLING TIME: 3 hours, 30 minutes

EQIPMENT: 8-inch square baking pan, blender or food processor

Ingredients:

FOR THE CRUST

- 1½ cups finely ground graham cracker crumbs (from about 9 graham crackers)
- ⅓ cup sugar
- 6 tablespoons (¾ stick) unsalted butter, melted

FOR THE FILLING

- 2 tablespoons water
- 2¼ teaspoons (1 envelope) unflavored gelatin
- 3 cups fresh raspberries, divided
- ½ cup sugar
- ¼ cup cream cheese, at room temperature
- 2 tablespoons low-fat or whole milk
- 1 tablespoon powdered sugar

Directions:

TO MAKE THE CRUST

1. Preheat the oven to 375°F.
2. In a medium bowl, stir together the graham cracker crumbs, sugar, and butter until well combined. Press the mixture into the bottom of an 8-inch baking pan in an even layer. Bake for about 7 minutes until lightly browned.
3. Remove from the oven and let cool.

TO MAKE THE FILLING

1. Put the water in a small bowl and sprinkle the gelatin over it. Let rest, stirring occasionally, until the gelatin fully dissolves. Prepare an ice bath by filling a large bowl with water and ice.
2. Meanwhile, in a blender or food processor, purée all but ½ cup of the raspberries until smooth. Transfer the purée to a medium saucepan set over medium heat.
3. Add the sugar and bring to a boil.
4. Add the gelatin mixture and cook for about 1 minute, stirring. Transfer the raspberry mixture to a medium bowl and set the bowl in the ice bath. Transfer the ice bath with the filling mixture to the refrigerator and chill for about 30 minutes, stirring once in a while with a rubber spatula, until the mixture is cool and thick.
5. While the raspberry mixture chills, in a medium bowl, combine the cream cheese, milk, and powdered sugar and, using an electric mixer or wooden spoon, beat until very smooth.
6. Spread the chilled raspberry filling over the prepared graham cracker crust and spoon the cream cheese mixture on top, placing dollops all over. Drag a knife through the cream cheese mixture to swirl it with the raspberry mixture. Top with the reserved raspberries. Refrigerate for about 3 hours, until fully set. Cut into 16 squares and serve chilled. Cover any leftovers with plastic wrap and refrigerate for up to 3 days.

SALTED CARAMEL–STUFFED FUDGE BROWNIES

Makes about 24 brownies

PREP TIME: 10 minutes

COOK TIME: 47 to 52 minutes

EQIPMENT: 9-by-13-inch baking pan

Ingredients:

- Nonstick baking spray
- 1½ cups all-purpose flour
- 1 teaspoon salt
- 1 teaspoon baking powder
- 2 cups sugar
- ¾ cup unsweetened cocoa powder
- 1 cup neutral-flavored oil (such as grapeseed, safflower, or sunflower seed)
- 4 eggs
- ¼ cup low-fat or whole milk
- 1 cup (6 ounces) semisweet chocolate chips
- 1 (11-ounce) package caramels or caramel pieces (such as Kraft Vanilla Caramels or Kraft Caramel Bits)
- 1 (14-ounce) can sweetened condensed milk
- 1 teaspoon coarse sea salt

Directions:

10. Preheat the oven to 350°F.

11. Line a 9-by-13-inch baking pan with parchment paper, and spray the parchment with baking spray.

12. In a medium bowl, stir together the flour, salt, and baking powder.

13. In a large bowl, with a wooden spoon or electric mixer, mix the sugar, cocoa powder, oil, eggs, and milk until well combined and smooth.

14. Add the flour mixture and stir or beat until incorporated.

15. Stir in the chocolate chips. Spoon ⅔ of the batter into the prepared pan and bake for 12 minutes.

16. Meanwhile, in a medium microwave-safe bowl, combine the caramels and sweetened condensed milk. Microwave at 50 percent power, in 30-second intervals, until the caramel melts and the mixture is smooth.

17. Remove the partially baked brownies from the oven and pour the melted caramel mixture over the top, spreading it into an even layer. Sprinkle the coarse sea salt over the caramel and then drop the remaining brownie batter on top in heaping spoonfuls. Using a butter knife, gently swirl together the caramel and brownie mixtures. Return to the oven and bake for 35 to 40 minutes more, until set and a toothpick inserted into the center comes out clean.

18. Remove from the oven and let the brownies cool completely before slicing and serving. Store in an airtight container at room temperature for up to 1 week.

STRAWBERRY CREAM PIE

Serves 6

PREP TIME: 20 minutes

CHILLING AND FREEZING TIME: 5 hours

EQIPMENT: 9-inch pie dish

Ingredients:

FOR THE CRUST

- 2¾ cups (about 11 ounces) crushed shortbread cookie crumbs
- 1 tablespoon sugar
- 6 tablespoons (¾ stick) unsalted butter, melted

FOR THE FILLING

- 1½ cups sliced fresh strawberries
- 2 tablespoons sugar
- ¾ cup mascarpone cheese, at room temperature
- ¾ cup plain Greek yogurt, at room temperature
- ¼ cup plus 2 tablespoons powdered sugar

Directions:

TO MAKE THE CRUST

1. In a medium bowl, stir together the cookie crumbs, sugar, and butter until thoroughly combined and beginning to clump. Press the mixture into the bottom and up the sides of a 9-inch pie dish, pressing firmly. Freeze for 1 hour.

TO MAKE THE FILLING

1. When the crust is frozen, put the strawberries in a medium bowl and toss with the sugar. Let the strawberries sit to macerate for 15 minutes.
2. While the strawberries sit, in a medium bowl, stir together the mascarpone, yogurt, and powdered sugar to mix well. Spread half the mascarpone-yogurt mixture in an even layer on top of the crust.
3. Layer half the strawberries on top and cover them with the remaining mascarpone-yogurt mixture. Arrange the remaining strawberries on top.
4. Refrigerate for at least 4 hours before slicing into wedges and serving.

MAPLE SYRUP CREAM PIE

Serves 8

PREP TIME: 10 minutes

CHILLING TIME: 4 hours

EQIPMENT: 9-inch pie dish, medium saucepan

Ingredients:

- 1½ cups maple syrup (see tip)
- 1 cup heavy (whipping) cream
- ¼ cup cornstarch mixed with ¼ cup cold water

- 1 (9-inch) piecrust (prebaked, homemade, or store-bought and baked according to the package Directions)

Directions:

1. In a medium saucepan set over medium-high heat, whisk the maple syrup and cream. Bring to a simmer.
2. Whisking constantly, add the cornstarch mixture. Still whisking constantly, bring the mixture to a boil and cook for about 2 minutes, lowering the heat if necessary to keep it from burning, until the mixture thickens. Pour the maple-cream mixture into the pie-crust and refrigerate for at least 4 hours until set. Serve chilled.

WITH SHORTBREAD CRUST

Serves 8

PREP TIME: 20 minutes

CHILLING TIME: 3 hours

EQIPMENT: 9-inch pie dish, electric mixer

Ingredients:

FOR THE CRUST

- 2¾ cups (about 11 ounces) crushed shortbread cookie crumbs
- 1 tablespoon sugar
- 6 tablespoons (¾ stick) unsalted butter, melted

FOR THE FILLING

- ⅔ cup sugar
- 2 eggs
- 2 ounces unsweetened baking chocolate, chopped
- ⅓ cup unsalted butter, left at room temperature for 15 to 20 minutes before using
- 1½ cups heavy (whipping) cream
- ¼ cup powdered sugar
- Chocolate shavings, for garnish

Directions:

TO MAKE THE CRUST

1. In large bowl, stir together the cookie crumbs, sugar, and butter until well combined. Press the mixture into the bottom and up the sides of 9-inch pie dish. Refrigerate for 1 hour before proceeding with the recipe.

TO MAKE THE FILLING

1. In a small saucepan, whisk the sugar and eggs until well mixed. Place the pan over medium heat and cook for about 4 minutes until the mixture is thick enough to coat the back of a spoon. Remove the pan from the heat and stir in the chocolate, stirring until it is completely melted and the mixture is smooth. Let cool for a few minutes.
2. Mix in the butter, stirring until it is fully incorporated. Transfer to a large bowl and refrigerate the mixture while you make the whipped cream.
3. In another large bowl, using a handheld electric mixer or a stand mixer, whip the cream until it holds soft peaks.
4. Add the powdered sugar and continue to whip until it holds stiff peaks. Add half the whipped cream to

the cooled chocolate mixture and gently fold it in with a rubber spatula. Pour the chocolate mixture into the prepared crust.

5. Dollop the remaining whipped cream on top and garnish with chocolate shavings. Refrigerate for at least 2 hours before serving.

MOCHA MUD PIE

Serves 8

PREP TIME: 20 minutes
CHILLING TIME: 4 hours, 30 minutes
EQIPMENT: 9-inch pie dish, electric mixer

Ingredients:

- 1 tablespoon instant espresso powder
- 1½ cups crushed chocolate wafer cookies (I prefer Nabisco Famous Chocolate Wafers)
- 6 tablespoons (¾ stick) unsalted butter, melted
- 3 ounces semisweet chocolate, chopped
- 2 cups heavy (whipping) cream
- ¾ cup powdered sugar, divided
- 1 (8-ounce) package cream cheese, at room temperature
- ½ teaspoon vanilla extract
- Chocolate shavings, for garnish
- 1 cup hot fudge sauce

Directions:

1. In a measuring cup, mix the espresso powder into ¼ cup water. Set aside to let the espresso powder dissolve.
2. In a medium bowl, stir together the chocolate wafer crumbs and butter until well combined. Press the mixture firmly into a 9-inch pie dish. Refrigerate for 30 minutes.
3. Meanwhile, in a small microwave-safe bowl, microwave the chocolate at 50 percent power, in 30-second intervals, stirring in between, until melted and smooth.
4. In a large bowl, with a handheld electric mixer or in a stand mixer, whip the heavy cream until it holds soft peaks. Add ½ cup of powdered sugar along with the vanilla. Whip until the mixture holds stiff peaks.
5. In another large bowl, beat together the cream cheese and remaining ¼ cup of powdered sugar until thoroughly combined.
6. Add the dissolved espresso powder and stir to incorporate completely.
7. Add the melted chocolate to the cream cheese mixture and mix to combine.
8. Gently fold 2 cups of whipped cream mixture into the cream cheese-and-chocolate mixture. Transfer to the prepared crust and smooth the top with a rubber spatula.
9. Spread the remaining whipped cream on top and garnish with chocolate shavings. Refrigerate the pie for at least 4 hours before serving.
10. Serve chilled with hot fudge sauce drizzled over the top.

SUGAR CREAM PIE

PREP TIME: 10 minutes
COOK TIME: 40 minutes
COOLING TIME: 1 hour
EQIPMENT: 9-inch pie dish
Ingredients:

- ½ cup granulated sugar
- ½ cup packed dark brown sugar
- 2 tablespoons all-purpose flour
- 2 cups heavy (whipping) cream
- ½ teaspoon vanilla extract
- 1 (9-inch) piecrust (prebaked, homemade, or store-bought and baked according to the package **Directions**)
- Powdered sugar, for dusting

Directions:

1. Preheat the oven to 400°F.
2. In a medium bowl, whisk the granulated sugar, brown sugar, and flour, breaking up any clumps.
3. In another medium bowl, stir together the cream and vanilla.
4. While whisking constantly, add the cream to the sugar mixture in a slow, steady stream. Whisk until the mixture is well combined and smooth. Pour the filling into the par-baked crust and bake the pie for about 40 minutes until the filling is set around the edges.
5. Remove the pie from the oven and set it on a wire rack to cool completely, at least 1 hour.
6. Sprinkle powdered sugar over the top of the pie, slice it into wedges, and serve at room temperature.

COCONUT CUSTARD PIE

Serves 8

PREP TIME: 5 minutes
COOK TIME: 50 minutes to 1 hour
COOLING AND **CHILLING TIME:** 5 hours
EQIPMENT: 9-inch pie dish
Ingredients:

- 6 tablespoons (¾ stick) unsalted butter, at room temperature, plus more for preparing the pie dish
- ½ cup all-purpose flour, plus more for preparing the pie dish
- 1 (14-ounce) can sweetened condensed milk
- 1 (13-ounce) can coconut milk
- 4 eggs
- 1½ cups sweetened, flaked coconut, divided
- 1 teaspoon vanilla extract
- ¼ teaspoon salt

Directions:

1. Preheat the oven to 350°F.

2. Grease a 9-inch pie dish with butter and dust it with flour.
3. In a large bowl, using an electric mixer or a whisk, or in a blender, combine the sweetened condensed milk, coconut milk, eggs, 1 cup of shredded coconut, butter, flour, vanilla, and salt. Beat until smooth. Pour the mixture into the prepared pie dish and bake for 50 minutes to 1 hour until the center is mostly set.
4. Remove from the oven and set the pie on a wire rack to cool to room temperature, about 1 hour. Transfer to the refrigerator and chill for at least 4 hours until completely set.
5. Just before serving, sprinkle the remaining coconut over the top. Cut into wedges and serve chilled.

DARK CHOCOLATE PECAN PIE

Serves 10

PREP TIME: 20 minutes
COOK TIME: 30 to 40 minutes
COOLING TIME: 2 hours
EQIPMENT: 9-inch pie dish, large rimmed baking sheet, small saucepan

Ingredients:

- 1½ cups pecan halves
- 6 tablespoons (¾ stick) unsalted butter
- 2 ounces bittersweet chocolate, chopped
- ¾ cup dark corn syrup
- 4 eggs
- ½ cup packed light brown sugar
- 1 tablespoon unsweetened cocoa powder
- 2 tablespoons bourbon
- ¼ teaspoon salt
- 1 (9-inch) piecrust (prebaked, homemade, or store-bought and baked according to the package **Directions**)

Directions:

1. Preheat the oven to 350°F.
2. Spread the pecans in a single layer on a large rimmed baking sheet and bake for 8 to 10 minutes.
3. Remove from the oven and let cool. Leave the oven on.
4. While the nuts cool, in a small saucepan set over low heat, combine the butter and chocolate. Cook, stirring constantly, until both are melted and the mixture is smooth. Remove from the heat and transfer the mixture to a large bowl. Let cool.
5. Add the corn syrup, eggs, brown sugar, cocoa powder, bourbon, and salt to the cooled chocolate mixture and whisk well to combine. Pour the filling into the crust and arrange the pecans in a single layer on top of the filling. Bake for 30 to 40 minutes, until the filling is just barely set.
6. Remove from the oven and place the pie on a wire rack to cool completely, at least 2 hours, before serving.

GINGER AND SPICE PUMPKIN PIE

Serves 8

PREP TIME: 10 minutes
COOK TIME: 40 to 50 minutes
EQIPMENT: 9-inch pie dish
Ingredients:

- 1 uncooked 9-inch piecrust (homemade or store-bought)
- 1 (15-ounce) can pumpkin purée
- ¾ cup sugar
- ¾ cup heavy (whipping) cream
- 2 eggs
- 1 tablespoon grated fresh ginger
- ½ teaspoon ground cinnamon
- ¼ teaspoon salt
- Pinch ground cloves
- Whipped cream, for serving

Directions:

1. Preheat the oven to 350°F.
2. Fit the piecrust into a 9-inch pie dish.
3. In a large bowl, whisk the pumpkin purée, sugar, cream, eggs, ginger, cinnamon, salt, and cloves until thoroughly combined. Spoon the mixture into the piecrust, smoothing the top with a rubber spatula. Bake for 40 to 50 minutes until just set in the center.
4. Remove from the oven and set the pie on a wire rack to cool to room temperature. Serve warm, dolloped with whipped cream.

TARTE TATIN

Serves 8

PREP TIME: 15 minutes
COOK TIME: 50 minutes
EQIPMENT: small saucepan, 9-inch round cake pan
Ingredients:

- All-purpose flour, for dusting the work surface
- 1 sheet (about 8 ounces) puff pastry
- 4 tablespoons salted butter
- 4 tablespoons sugar
- 6 Golden Delicious apples, peeled, cored, and cut into wedges
- Crème fraîche or vanilla ice cream, for serving

Directions:

1. Preheat the oven to 425°F.
2. On a lightly floured work surface, roll out the pastry sheet and trim it to fit a 9-inch round cake pan. Wrap the dough in plastic wrap and refrigerate until ready to use.
3. In a small saucepan set over medium heat, melt the butter.
4. Add the sugar, sprinkling it evenly over the butter. Cook for about 5 minutes, stirring occasionally, until

the mixture is golden brown. Remove the pan from the heat and pour the caramel into the cake pan, spreading it evenly over the bottom.

5. Arrange the apples in a single layer on top of the caramel. Bake for 30 minutes.

6. Remove the pan from the oven (leaving the oven on) and place the puff pastry on top of the apples. Use a sharp knife to cut 4 steam vents in the crust. Return to the oven and bake for about 20 minutes more until the pastry is golden brown.

7. Remove the pan from the oven and carefully invert the tart onto a wire rack. You may want to place a baking sheet underneath the rack to catch any messy caramel drips.

8. Cut into wedges and serve warm or at room temperature, topped with crème fraiche or vanilla ice cream.

WITH PASTRY CREAM

Makes 12 tartlets

PREP TIME: 20 minutes
COOK TIME: 18 to 22 minutes
CHILLING TIME: 2 hours
EQIPMENT: 12-cup muffin tin, 3½-inch round cookie cutter

Ingredients:

- All-purpose flour, for dusting the work surface
- 1 uncooked 9-inch piecrust (homemade or store-bought)
- 4 egg yolks
- ½ cup sugar
- ¼ cup cornstarch
- Pinch salt
- 2 cups low-fat or whole milk
- 1½ teaspoons vanilla extract
- Fresh fruit, for topping the tartlets (sliced peaches, nectarines, strawberries, raspberries, blueberries, or other fruit as desired)

Directions:

1. Preheat the oven to 400°F.

2. On a lightly floured work surface, Roll out the piecrust to an even thickness of about ⅛ inch. Using a 3½-inch round cookie cutter, cut out 12 dough circles. Fit the dough circles into the cups of a muffin tin, pressing them in to form little dough cups. Bake for 11 to 13 minutes until they are lightly golden brown. Transfer the cups to a wire rack to cool completely.

3. While the cups cool, make the filling. In a medium bowl, whisk the egg yolks until smooth.

4. In a saucepan set over medium heat, combine the sugar, cornstarch, and salt. Whisking continuously, add the milk in a slow, steady stream. Cook for about 5 minutes, whisking, until the mixture bubbles and thickens.

5. While whisking constantly, ladle about ⅓ of the milk mixture into the egg yolks. Transfer the egg yolk mixture to the saucepan, still whisking constantly, and bring to a boil. Cook for 2 to 4 minutes, whisking, until the mixture is very thick. Remove the saucepan from the heat and stir in the vanilla. Transfer the pastry cream to a bowl, cover with plastic wrap, and refrigerate for 2 hours.

6. Spoon, pipe, or scoop the pastry cream into the tart shells. Top with fresh fruit and serve immediately.

NECTARINE GALETTE

Serves 6

PREP TIME: 10 minutes

COOK TIME: 12 to 15 minutes

EQIPMENT: Baking sheet, pastry brush

Ingredients:

- 1 uncooked 9-inch piecrust (homemade or store-bought)
- 4 to 5 ripe nectarines, cut into wedges
- 3 tablespoons sugar, divided
- 1 tablespoon cornstarch
- 1 egg, beaten

Directions:

1. Preheat the oven to 425°F.
2. Line a baking sheet with parchment paper and lay the piecrust out on the prepared sheet.
3. In a medium bowl, toss together the nectarine slices, 2 tablespoons of sugar, and the cornstarch. Transfer the mixture to a colander over the sink and let it drain for a few minutes. Pour the fruit onto the piecrust, mounding it in the center and leaving a 2-inch border of crust all the way around the fruit.
4. Fold the uncovered sides of the crust up over the edges of the fruit and fold into pleats to make a rustic circle.
5. Brush the beaten egg over the crust and sprinkle the remaining tablespoon of sugar over the crust. Bake for 12 to 15 minutes until the crust is golden brown.
6. Remove from the oven and let cool. Serve warm or at room temperature.

CANNOLI CREAM–FILLED MINI TARTLETS

Makes 24 mini tartlets

PREP TIME: 20 minutes

COOK TIME: 11 to 13 minutes

CHILLING TIME: 30 minutes

EQIPMENT: 24-cup mini muffin tin, 2½-inch round cookie cutter

Ingredients:

- All-purpose flour, for dusting the work surface
- 1 uncooked 9-inch piecrust (homemade or store-bought)
- 12 ounces whole-milk ricotta cheese, drained
- 8 ounces mascarpone cheese
- ½ cup plus 2 tablespoons powdered sugar, plus more for dusting
- ½ cup mini semisweet chocolate chips

Directions:

1. Preheat the oven to 400°F.

2. On a lightly floured surface, roll out the piecrust to an even thickness of about ⅛ inch.

3. Using a 2½-inch round cookie cutter, cut out 24 dough circles. Fit the dough circles into the cups of a mini muffin tin, pressing them in to form little dough cups. Bake for 11 to 13 minutes until lightly golden brown. Transfer the cups to a wire rack to cool completely.

4. While the cups cool, make the filling. In a large bowl, with a rubber spatula, stir together the ricotta and mascarpone cheeses until well combined and smooth.

5. Add the powdered sugar and stir to incorporate well.

6. Stir in the chocolate chips and mix well. Cover and refrigerate for at least 30 minutes.

7. When ready to fill the cups, transfer the filling to a piping bag or a resealable plastic bag with the tip cut off one bottom corner. Pipe the filling into the pastry cups.

8. Dust with powdered sugar and serve. Cover and refrigerate any leftovers for up to 3 days.

SUGAR CREAM PIE

Serves 8

PREP TIME: 10 minutes
COOK TIME: 40 minutes
COOLING TIME: 1 hour
EQIPMENT: 9-inch pie dish
Ingredients:

- ½ cup granulated sugar
- ½ cup packed dark brown sugar
- 2 tablespoons all-purpose flour
- 2 cups heavy (whipping) cream
- ½ teaspoon vanilla extract
- 1 (9-inch) piecrust (prebaked, homemade, or store-bought and baked according to the package **Directions**)
- Powdered sugar, for dusting

Directions:

7. Preheat the oven to 400°F.

8. In a medium bowl, whisk the granulated sugar, brown sugar, and flour, breaking up any clumps.

9. In another medium bowl, stir together the cream and vanilla.

10. While whisking constantly, add the cream to the sugar mixture in a slow, steady stream. Whisk until the mixture is well combined and smooth. Pour the filling into the par-baked crust and bake the pie for about 40 minutes until the filling is set around the edges.

11. Remove the pie from the oven and set it on a wire rack to cool completely, at least 1 hour.

12. Sprinkle powdered sugar over the top of the pie, slice it into wedges, and serve at room temperature.

COCONUT CUSTARD PIE

Serves 8

PREP TIME: 5 minutes
COOK TIME: 50 minutes to 1 hour
COOLING AND **CHILLING TIME:** 5 hours

EQIPMENT: 9-inch pie dish

Ingredients:

- 6 tablespoons (¾ stick) unsalted butter, at room temperature, plus more for preparing the pie dish
- ½ cup all-purpose flour, plus more for preparing the pie dish
- 1 (14-ounce) can sweetened condensed milk
- 1 (13-ounce) can coconut milk
- 4 eggs
- 1½ cups sweetened, flaked coconut, divided
- 1 teaspoon vanilla extract
- ¼ teaspoon salt

Directions:

6. Preheat the oven to 350°F.
7. Grease a 9-inch pie dish with butter and dust it with flour.
8. In a large bowl, using an electric mixer or a whisk, or in a blender, combine the sweetened condensed milk, coconut milk, eggs, 1 cup of shredded coconut, butter, flour, vanilla, and salt. Beat until smooth. Pour the mixture into the prepared pie dish and bake for 50 minutes to 1 hour until the center is mostly set.
9. Remove from the oven and set the pie on a wire rack to cool to room temperature, about 1 hour. Transfer to the refrigerator and chill for at least 4 hours until completely set.
10. Just before serving, sprinkle the remaining coconut over the top. Cut into wedges and serve chilled.

DARK CHOCOLATE PECAN PIE

Serves 10

PREP TIME: 20 minutes

COOK TIME: 30 to 40 minutes

COOLING TIME: 2 hours

EQIPMENT: 9-inch pie dish, large rimmed baking sheet, small saucepan

Ingredients:

- 1½ cups pecan halves
- 6 tablespoons (¾ stick) unsalted butter
- 2 ounces bittersweet chocolate, chopped
- ¾ cup dark corn syrup
- 4 eggs
- ½ cup packed light brown sugar
- 1 tablespoon unsweetened cocoa powder
- 2 tablespoons bourbon
- ¼ teaspoon salt
- 1 (9-inch) piecrust (prebaked, homemade, or store-bought and baked according to the package **Directions**)

Directions:

7. Preheat the oven to 350°F.

8. Spread the pecans in a single layer on a large rimmed baking sheet and bake for 8 to 10 minutes.

9. Remove from the oven and let cool. Leave the oven on.

10. While the nuts cool, in a small saucepan set over low heat, combine the butter and chocolate. Cook, stirring constantly, until both are melted and the mixture is smooth. Remove from the heat and transfer the mixture to a large bowl. Let cool.

11. Add the corn syrup, eggs, brown sugar, cocoa powder, bourbon, and salt to the cooled chocolate mixture and whisk well to combine. Pour the filling into the crust and arrange the pecans in a single layer on top of the filling. Bake for 30 to 40 minutes, until the filling is just barely set.

12. Remove from the oven and place the pie on a wire rack to cool completely, at least 2 hours, before serving.

GINGER AND SPICE PUMPKIN PIE

Serves 8

PREP TIME: 10 minutes
COOK TIME: 40 to 50 minutes
EQIPMENT: 9-inch pie dish
Ingredients:

- 1 uncooked 9-inch piecrust (homemade or store-bought)
- 1 (15-ounce) can pumpkin purée
- ¾ cup sugar
- ¾ cup heavy (whipping) cream
- 2 eggs
- 1 tablespoon grated fresh ginger
- ½ teaspoon ground cinnamon
- ¼ teaspoon salt
- Pinch ground cloves
- Whipped cream, for serving

Directions:

5. Preheat the oven to 350°F.

6. Fit the piecrust into a 9-inch pie dish.

7. In a large bowl, whisk the pumpkin purée, sugar, cream, eggs, ginger, cinnamon, salt, and cloves until thoroughly combined. Spoon the mixture into the piecrust, smoothing the top with a rubber spatula. Bake for 40 to 50 minutes until just set in the center.

8. Remove from the oven and set the pie on a wire rack to cool to room temperature. Serve warm, dolloped with whipped cream.

TARTE TATIN

Serves 8

PREP TIME: 15 minutes
COOK TIME: 50 minutes
EQIPMENT: small saucepan, 9-inch round cake pan
Ingredients:

- All-purpose flour, for dusting the work surface
- 1 sheet (about 8 ounces) puff pastry
- 4 tablespoons salted butter
- 4 tablespoons sugar
- 6 Golden Delicious apples, peeled, cored, and cut into wedges
- Crème fraîche or vanilla ice cream, for serving

Directions:

9. Preheat the oven to 425°F.
10. On a lightly floured work surface, roll out the pastry sheet and trim it to fit a 9-inch round cake pan. Wrap the dough in plastic wrap and refrigerate until ready to use.
11. In a small saucepan set over medium heat, melt the butter.
12. Add the sugar, sprinkling it evenly over the butter. Cook for about 5 minutes, stirring occasionally, until the mixture is golden brown. Remove the pan from the heat and pour the caramel into the cake pan, spreading it evenly over the bottom.
13. Arrange the apples in a single layer on top of the caramel. Bake for 30 minutes.
14. Remove the pan from the oven (leaving the oven on) and place the puff pastry on top of the apples. Use a sharp knife to cut 4 steam vents in the crust. Return to the oven and bake for about 20 minutes more until the pastry is golden brown.
15. Remove the pan from the oven and carefully invert the tart onto a wire rack. You may want to place a baking sheet underneath the rack to catch any messy caramel drips.
16. Cut into wedges and serve warm or at room temperature, topped with crème fraiche or vanilla ice cream.

WITH PASTRY CREAM

Makes 12 tartlets

PREP TIME: 20 minutes
COOK TIME: 18 to 22 minutes
CHILLING TIME: 2 hours
EQIPMENT: 12-cup muffin tin, 3½-inch round cookie cutter

Ingredients:

- All-purpose flour, for dusting the work surface
- 1 uncooked 9-inch piecrust (homemade or store-bought)
- 4 egg yolks
- ½ cup sugar
- ¼ cup cornstarch
- Pinch salt
- 2 cups low-fat or whole milk
- 1½ teaspoons vanilla extract
- Fresh fruit, for topping the tartlets (sliced peaches, nectarines, strawberries, raspberries, blueberries, or other fruit as desired)

Directions:

7. Preheat the oven to 400°F.

8. On a lightly floured work surface, Roll out the piecrust to an even thickness of about ⅛ inch. Using a 3½-inch round cookie cutter, cut out 12 dough circles. Fit the dough circles into the cups of a muffin tin, pressing them in to form little dough cups. Bake for 11 to 13 minutes until they are lightly golden brown. Transfer the cups to a wire rack to cool completely.

9. While the cups cool, make the filling. In a medium bowl, whisk the egg yolks until smooth.

10. In a saucepan set over medium heat, combine the sugar, cornstarch, and salt. Whisking continuously, add the milk in a slow, steady stream. Cook for about 5 minutes, whisking, until the mixture bubbles and thickens.

11. While whisking constantly, ladle about ⅓ of the milk mixture into the egg yolks. Transfer the egg yolk mixture to the saucepan, still whisking constantly, and bring to a boil. Cook for 2 to 4 minutes, whisking, until the mixture is very thick. Remove the saucepan from the heat and stir in the vanilla. Transfer the pastry cream to a bowl, cover with plastic wrap, and refrigerate for 2 hours.

12. Spoon, pipe, or scoop the pastry cream into the tart shells. Top with fresh fruit and serve immediately.

TANGY LEMON BARS

Makes about 30 bars

PREP TIME: 10 minutes
CHILLING TIME: Overnight
EQIPMENT: 9-by-13-inch baking pan
Ingredients:

- 10 graham crackers, crushed
- 2 teaspoons lemon zest
- Juice of 2½ lemons
- 1 (14-ounce) can sweetened condensed milk
- 1½ cups powdered sugar, plus more for dusting
- 3 tablespoons unsalted butter, melted
- 3 tablespoons low-fat or whole milk

Directions:

1. Line the bottom of a 9-by-13-inch baking pan with the crushed graham crackers.

2. In a medium bowl, whisk the lemon zest, lemon juice, and sweetened condensed milk until well combined. Pour the mixture evenly over the graham crackers.

3. In another medium bowl, stir together the powdered sugar, butter, and milk until well combined. Pour that mixture over the lemon juice mixture in the pan. Cover the pan and refrigerate overnight.

4. To serve, dust the top generously with powdered sugar, cut into 2-inch squares, and serve. Cover any leftovers with plastic wrap and keep refrigerated for up to 3 days.

PB& J BARS

Makes about 30 bars

PREP TIME: 10 minutes
COOK TIME: 35 minutes
EQIPMENT: 9-by-13-inch baking pan
Ingredients:

- 1 cup (2 sticks) unsalted butter, melted, plus more for preparing the baking pan
- 2¼ cups all-purpose flour
- ½ teaspoon salt
- ½ teaspoon baking soda
- ¼ teaspoon baking powder
- 1 cup packed dark brown sugar
- ½ cup granulated sugar
- 1½ cups crunchy peanut butter
- 2 eggs, lightly beaten
- 2 teaspoons vanilla extract
- 1 cup fruit jam or preserves of choice

Directions:

1. Preheat the oven to 350°F.
2. Generously grease a 9-by-13-inch baking pan with butter.
3. In a medium bowl, whisk the flour, salt, baking soda, and baking powder.
4. In a large bowl, with a wooden spoon or rubber spatula, stir together the brown sugar, granulated sugar, and melted butter, mashing the sugar into the butter as you stir, until the mixture is smooth and creamy.
5. Add the peanut butter and stir until the mixture is smooth and well combined.
6. Stir in the eggs and vanilla until incorporated.
7. Add the flour mixture and stir until combined. Transfer the batter to the prepared pan.
8. Using the back of a spoon, make little wells, evenly spaced, all over the top of the batter. Fill each well with a spoonful of jam or preserves. With a knife, swirl the jam through the batter. Bake for about 35 minutes, until a toothpick inserted in the center comes out clean.
9. Remove from the oven and set the pan on a wire rack to cool completely for about 1 hour.
10. Cut into 2-inch squares and serve immediately or wrap in plastic wrap and store at room temperature for up to 5 days.

COOKIES 'N ' CREAM BARS

Makes about 30 bars

PREP TIME: 10 minutes

CHILLING TIME: 2 hours

EQIPMENT: 9-inch square baking pan

Ingredients:

FOR THE CRUST

- 24 cream-filled chocolate sandwich cookies, finely crushed
- ¼ cup (½ stick) unsalted butter, melted

FOR THE FILLING

- ¾ cup white chocolate chips
- 6 ounces cream cheese, at room temperature
- 12 cream-filled chocolate sandwich cookies, coarsely chopped

FOR THE TOPPING

- 6 cream-filled chocolate sandwich cookies, coarsely chopped
- ¾ cup semisweet chocolate chips

Directions:

TO MAKE THE CRUST

1. Line a 9-inch square baking pan with parchment paper.
2. In a medium bowl, stir together the cookie crumbs and butter until well combined. Press the mixture into the bottom of the prepared pan.

TO MAKE THE FILLING

1. In a medium microwave-safe bowl, microwave the white chocolate at 50 percent power, in 30-second intervals, stirring in between, until completely melted and smooth.
2. Add the cream cheese and stir until smooth.
3. Add the chopped cookies and stir to mix. Spread the filling evenly over the crust.

TO MAKE THE TOPPING

1. Sprinkle the chopped cookies evenly over the filling.
2. In a small microwave-safe bowl, microwave the chocolate chips at 50 percent power, at 30-second intervals, stirring in between, until melted and smooth. Drizzle the melted chocolate over the top. Cover and refrigerate for at least 2 hours until firm and set.
3. Slice into 2-inch squares and serve. Cover any remaining bars with plastic wrap and keep refrigerated for up to 3 days.

BLUEBERRY CHEESECAKE BARS

Makes about 16 bars

PREP TIME: 15 minutes

CHILLING TIME: 2 hours

EQIPMENT: 8-inch square baking pan

Ingredients:

FOR THE CRUST

- 10 graham crackers, crushed (about 2 cups)
- ¼ cup sugar
- ½ cup (1 stick) unsalted butter, melted

FOR THE FILLING

- 2 (8-ounce) packages cream cheese, at room temperature
- 1 cup powdered sugar
- 2 cups heavy (whipping) cream
- 1 teaspoon vanilla extract

FOR THE SAUCE

- 2 cups fresh or frozen blueberries
- ½ cup sugar
- 1 tablespoon unsalted butter
- 2 teaspoons cornstarch
- 1 teaspoon vanilla extract

Directions:

TO MAKE THE CRUST

1. In a medium bowl, stir together the crushed graham crackers, sugar, and butter until well combined. Press the mixture into an 8-inch square baking pan in an even layer.

TO MAKE THE FILLING

1. In a large bowl, using either a stand mixer with a whisk attachment or a handheld mixer or whisk, whisk the cream cheese and powdered sugar until smooth.

2. Whisk in the cream and vanilla and continue whisking for several minutes until the mixture thickens. Pour the filling over the crust. Cover and refrigerate for at least 2 hours, until firm.

TO MAKE THE SAUCE

1. In a medium saucepan set over medium-high heat, combine the blueberries, sugar, butter, cornstarch, and vanilla. Cover and cook for about 5 minutes until the blueberries break down and the sauce thickens. Remove from the heat and let cool. Refrigerate until ready to serve.

2. To serve, pour the blueberry sauce over the chilled cheesecake, cut into squares, and serve. Cover any leftovers with plastic wrap and keep refrigerated for up to 3 days.

CARAMEL FLAN

Serves 4

PREP TIME: 20 minutes

COOK TIME: 45 minutes

CHILLING TIME: 3 hours

EQIPMENT: 4 (6-ounce) ramekins, a deep baking dish large enough to hold the ramekins, 2 saucepans, fine-mesh sieve

Ingredients:

FOR THE CARAMEL

- Unsalted butter, for preparing the ramekins
- ½ cup sugar
- 5 tablespoons boiling water

FOR THE CUSTARD

- 4 egg yolks
- 2 eggs
- ¼ cup sugar, divided
- 1½ cups low-fat or whole milk
- 1 teaspoon vanilla extract

Directions:

TO MAKE THE CARAMEL

1. Preheat the oven to 275°F.
2. Lightly grease the ramekins with butter.
3. In a small saucepan over medium heat, heat the sugar for about 5 minutes, tilting and swirling the pan until it is completely melted and lightly browned.
4. Carefully add the boiling water. Swirl the pan until the water and caramel are well combined. Remove

from the heat.

5. Divide the caramel mixture evenly among the prepared ramekins, tilting the ramekins to ensure that the caramel evenly coats the entire bottom of each. Place the ramekins into the baking dish and fill the dish with enough water to come about 2 inches up the sides of the ramekins.

TO MAKE THE CUSTARD

1. In a medium bowl, whisk the egg yolks, eggs, and 2½ tablespoons of sugar.
2. In a clean saucepan set over medium-low heat, combine the milk and the remaining 1½ tablespoons of sugar. When the milk just begins to boil, pour it into a spouted measuring cup.
3. While whisking the eggs constantly, add the milk in a slow, steady stream until the mixture is well combined. Strain the mixture through a fine-mesh sieve into a bowl.
4. Pour or ladle the mixture into the ramekins, dividing evenly. Cover the baking pan with aluminum foil and carefully transfer it to the oven. Bake for 45 minutes.
5. Remove the pan from the oven, but leave the foil cover on until the custards cool completely.
6. Transfer the foil-covered baking dish to the refrigerator and chill the custards for at least 3 hours.
7. To serve, run a thin-bladed knife around the inside of each ramekin to loosen the custard. Place a serving plate over one of the ramekins and carefully invert it to unmold the custard. If the custard fails to release from the ramekin, leave the ramekin upside down on the plate. As the custard warms and gravity asserts itself, the custard should release. Serve immediately. Cover any leftovers with plastic wrap and refrigerate for up to 3 days.

CHERRY-VANILLA FROZEN YOGURT

Serves 8

PREP TIME: 20 minutes

CHILLING TIME: 3 hours

EQIPMENT: Medium saucepan, blender, freezer-safe storage container

Ingredients:

- 3 cups pitted fresh cherries
- ¾ cup sugar
- 2 tablespoons freshly squeezed lemon juice
- 1½ cups full-fat plain yogurt
- ¼ cup whole milk
- 1 tablespoon vanilla extract

Directions:

1. In a medium saucepan set over medium-high heat, combine the cherries, sugar, and lemon juice, stirring until the mixture simmers and the sugar fully dissolves. Remove from the heat and let cool for 10 minutes.
2. Transfer the cherry mixture to a blender and process until smooth.
3. Add the yogurt, milk, and vanilla. Pulse to mix well. Pour the mixture into a freezer-safe storage container, cover with plastic wrap, and freeze for about 45 minutes before checking on it the first time. As soon as it begins to freeze around the edges, mix it vigorously with a whisk, spatula, wooden spoon, or ideally, a handheld electric mixer or immersion blender. Continue to freeze, mixing it every 30 minutes, until it is fully frozen, about 3 hours total.
4. Keep frozen until ready to serve.

BUTTERMINTS

Makes about 1 pound

PREP TIME: 15 minutes

DRYING TIME: 12 hours

EQIPMENT: Baking sheet, electric mixer

Ingredients:

- ½ cup (1 stick) unsalted butter, removed from the refrigerator about 15 minutes before using
- 2 tablespoons heavy (whipping) cream
- 1 teaspoon peppermint extract
- Pinch salt
- 3¾ cups powdered sugar, divided, plus more for dusting your hands

Directions:

1. Line a large baking sheet with parchment paper.
2. In a large bowl, using an electric mixer or in a stand mixer fitted with a whisk attachment set on high speed, beat the butter until it is fluffy and light. With a rubber spatula, scrape down the sides of the bowl.
3. Add the cream, peppermint extract, and salt. Beat to combine thoroughly.
4. Add 1½ cups of powdered sugar and beat on low speed until combined. Add another 1½ cups of powdered sugar and mix until thoroughly incorporated. Add the remaining ¾ cup of powdered sugar and beat until incorporated. Raise the mixer speed to high and beat for about 4 minutes until the mixture becomes very airy and light.
5. Coat your hands lightly with powdered sugar and pick up the dough ball, rolling it between your hands to make a rope about as thick as your thumb. Using a sharp knife, cut the rope into ¾-inch-long pieces. Arrange the mints on the prepared sheet in a single layer. Leave the baking sheet out, uncovered, at room temperature for about 12 hours until the candies are dry. Serve immediately or refrigerate in an airtight container for up to 1 week.

HOMEMADE CARAMELS

Makes 64 (1-inch) caramels

PREP TIME: 10 minutes

COOK TIME: 10 minutes

COOLING TIME: 1 to 2 hours

EQIPMENT: 8-inch square baking pan

Ingredients:

- ¾ cup (1½ sticks) unsalted butter
- ½ cup sugar
- 3 tablespoons light corn syrup
- 1 (14-ounce) can sweetened condensed milk
- ¼ teaspoon salt
- ½ teaspoon vanilla extract

Directions:

1. Line an 8-inch square baking pan with aluminum foil.
2. In a medium saucepan set over medium heat, stir together the butter and sugar. When the butter is completely melted, add the corn syrup, sweetened condensed milk, and salt. Stir to combine.
3. Raise the heat to medium-high and bring the mixture to a boil. Lower the heat and let the mixture cook for about 10 minutes (it should be bubbling vigorously), stirring constantly, until it turns a deep golden brown. At this point, the caramel should be pulling away from the sides of the pan as you stir. Remove the pan from the heat and immediately stir in the vanilla.
4. Transfer the caramel to the prepared baking pan and let cool completely, 1 to 2 hours.
5. Cut the cooled caramel into squares and serve immediately, or wrap in wax paper and store at room temperature for up to 2 weeks.

HONEYCOMB CANDY

Serves 8

PREP TIME: 5 minutes
COOK TIME: 10 minutes
COOLING TIME: 30 minutes
EQIPMENT: Medium saucepan, baking sheet
Ingredients:
- ¼ cup plus 1 tablespoon sugar
- ¼ cup honey
- Pinch salt
- 1½ teaspoons baking soda

Directions:
1. Line a baking sheet with parchment paper.
2. In a medium saucepan set over medium-high heat, stir together the sugar, honey, and salt. Bring to a boil. Cook for about 10 minutes, stirring frequently, until the mixture turns deep golden brown. Remove the pan from the heat and quickly stir in the baking soda. Be careful as the mixture will bubble and foam up dramatically. Stir until the baking soda dissolves completely.
3. Pour the mixture onto the prepared sheet and let cool to room temperature, about 30 minutes. When cool, it will be fully set.
4. Break into pieces to serve.

HONEYCOMB CANDY

Serves 8

PREP TIME: 5 minutes
COOK TIME: 10 minutes
COOLING TIME: 30 minutes
EQIPMENT: Medium saucepan, baking sheet
Ingredients:
- ¼ cup plus 1 tablespoon sugar
- ¼ cup honey
- Pinch salt

- 1½ teaspoons baking soda

Directions:

5. Line a baking sheet with parchment paper.

6. In a medium saucepan set over medium-high heat, stir together the sugar, honey, and salt. Bring to a boil. Cook for about 10 minutes, stirring frequently, until the mixture turns deep golden brown. Remove the pan from the heat and quickly stir in the baking soda. Be careful as the mixture will bubble and foam up dramatically. Stir until the baking soda dissolves completely.

7. Pour the mixture onto the prepared sheet and let cool to room temperature, about 30 minutes. When cool, it will be fully set.

8. Break into pieces to serve.

PEANUT BRITTLE

Serves 10

PREP TIME: 20 minutes

COOLING TIME: 1 to 2 hours

EQIPMENT: Baking sheet

Ingredients:

- Nonstick baking spray
- 1 cup sugar
- ½ cup light corn syrup
- 1 cup unsalted peanuts
- ¼ teaspoon salt
- 1 tablespoon unsalted butter
- 1 teaspoon vanilla extract
- 1 teaspoon baking soda

Directions:

1. Spray a baking sheet with nonstick baking spray.

2. In a large microwave-safe bowl, whisk the sugar and corn syrup. Microwave at full power for 4 minutes.

3. Stir in the peanuts and salt to combine. Microwave again at full power for 3½ minutes.

4. Stir in the butter and vanilla until the butter melts completely. Return to the microwave and microwave at full power for 1½ minutes more.

5. Immediately stir in the baking soda. The mixture will foam up. Transfer the mixture to the prepared sheet, and with a rubber spatula, gently spread it into an even layer.

6. Let cool completely for 1 to 2 hours. To serve, break the brittle into pieces.

MIMOSA JELLY CANDIES

Makes 64 (1-inch) candies

PREP TIME: 5 minutes

COOK TIME: 30 minutes

CHILLING AND SETTING TIME: 28 to 52 hours

EQIPMENT: 8-inch square baking pan

Ingredients:

- Nonstick baking spray
- 3 tablespoons unflavored gelatin (about 4 envelopes)
- 3 cups sugar, plus more for coating the candies
- ¼ to ½ teaspoon orange flavoring oil
- ¼ to ½ teaspoon champagne flavoring oil
- Orange food coloring, for coloring the candies

Directions:

8. Line an 8-inch square baking pan with plastic wrap (let the plastic wrap hang over the sides of the pan for easy removal) and spray with nonstick baking spray.

9. Put ¾ cup cold water into a medium saucepan, sprinkle the gelatin evenly over the top, and let sit for 5 minutes.

10. In another pot or a kettle, bring 1 cup plus 2 tablespoons water to a boil. Once the gelatin has been sitting in the cold water for 5 minutes, add the boiling water to the saucepan. Stir the mixture until the gelatin dissolves completely.

11. Add the sugar and stir to combine. Place the saucepan over medium-high heat and bring the mixture to a boil. Lower the heat to medium and simmer for 25 minutes, stirring constantly. Remove the pan from the heat.

12. Stir in the orange and champagne flavoring oils to taste. Add orange food coloring to your desired color. Pour the hot mixture into the prepared pan. Cover with plastic wrap and refrigerate for at least 4 hours until completely set.

13. Lift the set jelly from the pan using the plastic wrap. Peel off the plastic and dredge the whole jelly in sugar, coating it evenly. Using a sharp knife sprayed with nonstick baking spray, cut the jelly into small squares (½ inch to 1 inch). Roll the cut candies in the sugar to coat the cut edges and place them in a single layer on parchment paper.

14. Let sit, uncovered, at room temperature for 24 to 48 hours, until the sugar crystalizes. Store in an airtight container at room temperature for up to 3 weeks.

MEXICAN COCONUT CANDY SQUARES

Makes 64 (1-inch) candies

PREP TIME: 10 minutes
CHILLING TIME: 1 hour
EQIPMENT: 8-inch square baking pan
Ingredients:

- 2 egg whites, lightly beaten
- 2 cups powdered sugar
- 1 cup shredded, unsweetened coconut
- ½ teaspoon vanilla extract
- 1 cup coconut oil
- Red or pink food coloring, for coloring the candies

Directions:

1. Line an 8-inch square baking pan with parchment paper.
2. In a medium bowl, stir together the beaten egg whites, powdered sugar, shredded coconut, and vanilla.
3. In a small saucepan set over low heat, melt the coconut oil. Stir the melted coconut oil into the sugar-and-coconut mixture. Transfer half the mixture to the prepared pan, pressing it down and smoothing the top into an even layer.
4. Add a few drops of food coloring to the remaining mixture and stir to blend the color. Pour the pink mixture on top of the mixture in the pan and press down, smoothing the top. Refrigerate for at least 1 hour until completely set.
5. Cut into 1-inch squares to serve.

CANDY-COATED POPCORN

Makes 10 cups

PREP TIME: 5 minutes

COOKING TIME: 5 minutes

SETTING TIME: 30 minutes

EQIPMENT: Medium saucepan

Ingredients:

- 10 cups popped popcorn (from about ⅔ cup kernels) or 1 to 2 bags microwave popcorn
- ½ cup (1 stick) unsalted butter
- ⅔ cup sugar
- ⅓ cup corn syrup
- 1 teaspoon vanilla extract
- Food coloring (optional)

Directions:

4. Place the popcorn in a large bowl and set aside.
5. In a medium saucepan set over medium heat, stir together the butter, sugar, corn syrup, and vanilla until the butter and sugar completely dissolve. Bring to a boil. Remove from the heat and stir in the food coloring (if using).
6. Pour the mixture over the popcorn and toss to coat well. Let cool for about 30 minutes. Serve immediately or store in an airtight container at room temperature for up to 1 week.

RAINBOW ROCK CANDY

Makes about 30 pieces

PREP TIME: 5 minutes

COOK TIME: 30 minutes

EQIPMENT: Baking sheet, candy thermometer (recommended, but not required)

Ingredients:

- Nonstick baking spray
- 2 cups sugar
- ½ cup light corn syrup

- ½ teaspoon flavoring oil of your choice
- Food coloring, for coloring the candies
- Powdered sugar, for dusting

Directions:

2. Coat a baking sheet with nonstick bak

6. ing spray.

7. In a large saucepan set over medium-high heat, stir together the sugar, corn syrup, and ½ cup water. Bring to a boil. Cook for 20 to 30 minutes. If using a candy thermometer, cook the mixture until it reaches 300°F. If you are not using a candy thermometer, test the temperature by dropping a teaspoon or so of the mixture into a glass of ice water. When it is up to temperature, it will harden and become crunchy immediately.

8. Remove the pan from the heat and add the flavoring oil and food coloring as desired. You can split this mixture into batches and add different flavors and colors to each batch if desired.

9. Transfer the hot mixture to the prepared sheet and let it spread into an even layer. Let cool for about 30 minutes until hardened.

10. Remove the candy sheet from the pan and dust it with powdered sugar. Break the candy into pieces. Store in an airtight container at room temperature for up to 1 month.

CHOCOLATE-DIPPED S'MORES MARSHMALLOW BONBONS

Makes about 40 pieces

PREP TIME: 20 minutes

CHILLING TIME: 30 minutes

EQIPMENT: Large rimmed baking sheet, skewer

Ingredients:

- 40 marshmallows
- 12 ounces semisweet chocolate, chopped
- 2 tablespoons coconut oil
- 1½ cups finely crushed graham cracker crumbs

Directions:

7. Cover a large rimmed baking sheet with parchment paper.

8. Arrange the marshmallows on the prepared baking sheet in a single layer and place in the freezer while you prepare the coatings.

9. In a medium microwave-safe bowl, combine the chocolate and coconut oil. Microwave at 50 percent power, in 30-second intervals, stirring in between, until the chocolate is completely melted and the mixture is smooth.

10. Place the graham cracker crumbs in a wide, shallow bowl for dipping.

11. Use a skewer or toothpick to spear one of the chilled marshmallows and dip it first in the chocolate mixture to coat well and then in the graham cracker crumbs. Once coated, slide the marshmallow off the skewer and back onto the parchment-covered sheet, using a fork, if needed, to slide it off the skewer without disturbing the coating.

12. Refrigerate for about 30 minutes until the chocolate is completely set.

DARK CHOCOLATE, CHERRY, AND HAZELNUT BARK

Serves 12

PREP TIME: 5 minutes

CHILLING TIME: 30 minutes

EQIPMENT: Rimmed baking sheet

Ingredients:

- 12 ounces semisweet chocolate, chopped, or 1 (12-ounce) bag semisweet chocolate chips
- 1 cup toasted hazelnuts, chopped
- ½ cup dried cherries

Directions:

6. Line a rimmed baking sheet with parchment paper.

7. Dump the chocolate into the prepared baking pan and spread it into an even layer. Place the pan in a cold oven and turn the heat to 350°F. Bake for 6 to 8 minutes, until the chocolate is soft and mostly melted.

8. Remove from the oven and use a knife or a rubber spatula to swirl and spread the chocolate around, which will help it melt completely.

9. While the chocolate is still warm and melty, sprinkle the chopped hazelnuts and dried cherries over the top. Refrigerate for about 30 minutes until set.

10. To serve, remove from the refrigerator and break it into pieces. Store leftovers in a covered container at room temperature.

S'MORES CHOCOLATE BARK

Serves 12

PREP TIME: 15 minutes

CHILLING TIME: 1 hour

EQIPMENT: 8-by-11-inch baking pan

Ingredients:

- 12 ounces milk chocolate, chopped, or 1 (12-ounce) bag milk chocolate chips
- 4 to 6 graham crackers, broken into small pieces
- 1 cup mini marshmallows
- ½ cup white chocolate chips
- 1 cup marshmallow cream

Directions:

8. Line an 8-by-11-inch baking pan with parchment paper.

9. Put the milk chocolate into the prepared pan and spread it into an even layer. Place the pan in a cold oven and turn the heat to 350°F. Bake for 6 to 8 minutes until the chocolate is soft and mostly melted.

10. Remove from the oven and use a knife or a rubber spatula to swirl and spread the chocolate around, which will help it melt completely.

11. While the chocolate is still warm and melty, sprinkle the graham cracker pieces and marshmallows over

the top. Refrigerate for about 30 minutes until set.

12. While the milk chocolate layer chills, in a medium microwave-safe bowl, microwave the white chocolate chips at 50 percent power, in 30-second intervals, stirring in between, until fully melted and smooth.

13. Add the marshmallow cream and microwave again at 50 percent power, in 30-second intervals, stirring in between, until the mixture is smooth. Immediately spread the marshmallow layer over the set chocolate layer. Refrigerate for about 30 minutes until completely set.

14. To serve, break the bark into pieces. Store refrigerated in a covered container.

WITH FLAKY SEA SALT

Makes 12 cupcakes

PREP TIME: 10 minutes

BAKE TIME: 18 to 20 minutes

EQIPMENT: 12-cup muffin tin, paper cupcake liners

Ingredients:

FOR THE CUPCAKES

- 1½ cups all-purpose flour
- 1½ teaspoons baking powder
- ¼ teaspoon salt
- ½ cup (1 stick) unsalted butter, at room temperature
- ¼ cup granulated sugar
- ½ cup packed dark brown sugar
- 1 teaspoon vanilla extract
- 2 eggs
- ½ cup low-fat or whole milk

FOR THE FROSTING

- ½ cup (1 stick) unsalted butter, at room temperature
- 1 cup packed dark brown sugar
- ⅓ cup heavy (whipping) cream
- ½ teaspoon salt
- 2 to 2½ cups powdered sugar
- 1 teaspoon flaky sea salt

Directions:

TO MAKE THE CUPCAKES

1. Preheat the oven to 350°F.

2. Line a 12-cup muffin tin with paper liners.

3. In a medium bowl, combine the flour, baking powder, and salt.

4. In a large bowl, with a handheld electric mixer or stand mixer, cream together the butter, granulated sugar, and brown sugar for about 3 minutes until pale and fluffy.

5. Add the vanilla and eggs and beat to combine.

6. Add the dry ingredients and the milk in alternating batches, beating to combine after each addition.

Scoop the batter into the prepared muffin tin. Bake for 18 to 20 minutes until a toothpick inserted into the center of one of the cupcakes comes out clean.

7. Remove from the oven and let the cupcakes cool in the pan for a few minutes before removing them from the tin to a wire rack to cool completely.

TO MAKE THE FROSTING

1. While the cupcakes cool, make the frosting. In a small saucepan over medium heat, melt the butter. Add the brown sugar, cream, and salt. Cook for about 4 minutes, stirring, until the sugar dissolves completely. Remove from the heat and let cool.

2. In a large bowl, using a handheld electric mixer or in a stand mixer, combine the brown sugar mixture with 2 cups of powdered sugar and beat on medium speed for 5 minutes until thick. Add more powdered sugar as needed to get a thick, spreadable consistency.

3. When the cupcakes are cool, pipe, spread, or scoop the frosting onto them.

4. Sprinkle with flaky sea salt to garnish. Serve at room temperature.

WITH WHITE CHOCOLATE–ORANGE BUTTERCREAM

Makes 12 cupcakes

PREP TIME: 30 minutes

COOK TIME: 18 to 20 minutes

EQIPMENT: 12-cup muffin tin, paper cupcake liners (preferably dark pink in color)

Ingredients:

FOR THE CUPCAKES

- 1 cup all-purpose flour
- ¾ cup unsweetened Dutch process cocoa powder
- 1 teaspoon baking powder
- ¼ teaspoon salt
- ½ cup (1 stick) unsalted butter, at room temperature
- 1 cup plus 3 tablespoons sugar, divided
- 2 teaspoons vanilla extract
- 2 eggs
- ½ cup sour cream
- Juice of 1 orange (see tip)

FOR THE BUTTERCREAM

- 2 ounces white chocolate
- 5 tablespoons unsalted butter, at room temperature
- 2 cups powdered sugar
- Zest of 1 orange

Directions:

TO MAKE THE CUPCAKES

1. Preheat the oven to 350°F.

2. Line a 12-cup muffin tin with dark pink paper liners.

3. In a medium bowl, stir together the flour, cocoa powder, baking powder, and salt.

4. In a large bowl, using an electric mixer or in a stand mixer, beat together the butter and 1 cup of sugar on high speed until light and fluffy.

5. Add the vanilla, eggs, and sour cream and beat until incorporated.

6. Add the flour mixture in 2 batches, beating after each addition until incorporated. Scoop the batter into the prepared muffin tin and bake for 18 to 20 minutes until a toothpick inserted into the center of one of the cupcakes comes out clean.

7. Remove from the oven and let the cupcakes cool for a couple of minutes before removing them from the tin to a wire rack to cool completely.

8. Meanwhile, in a small bowl, stir together the orange juice and remaining 3 tablespoons of sugar. Drizzle the mixture over the warm cupcakes and let them cool completely.

TO MAKE THE BUTTERCREAM

1. In a small microwave-safe bowl, microwave the white chocolate at 50 percent power, in 30-second intervals, stirring in between, until completely melted and smooth.

2. In a medium bowl, beat the butter until light and fluffy.

3. Add the powdered sugar to the butter in 2 or 3 batches, beating after each addition until well combined. Continue to beat for about 5 minutes until thick and smooth.

4. Add the melted chocolate and orange zest and beat to incorporate.

5. Pipe, spread, or scoop the frosting onto the cooled cupcakes.

RED VELVET CUPCAKES

Makes 12 cupcakes

PREP TIME: 20 minutes

COOK TIME: 18 to 20 minutes

EQIPMENT: 12-cup muffin tin, paper cupcake liners

Ingredients:

FOR THE CUPCAKES

- 4 tablespoons (½ stick) unsalted butter, at room temperature
- ¾ cup sugar
- 1 egg
- 2½ tablespoons unsweetened cocoa powder
- 3 tablespoons red food coloring
- ½ teaspoon vanilla extract
- ½ cup buttermilk
- 1 cup plus 2 tablespoons all-purpose flour
- 1½ teaspoons distilled white vinegar
- ½ teaspoon salt
- ½ teaspoon baking soda

FOR THE FROSTING

- ½ cup (1 stick) unsalted butter, at room temperature

- 4 ounces cream cheese, at room temperature
- 2½ cups powdered sugar
- 1 tablespoon vanilla extract

Directions:

TO MAKE THE CUPCAKES

1. Preheat the oven to 350°F.
2. Line a 12-cup muffin tin with paper liners.
3. In a large bowl, with a handheld electric mixer or in a stand mixer, cream together the butter and sugar on medium speed for about 3 minutes until the mixture becomes pale and fluffy.
4. Add the egg and beat on high speed to incorporate.
5. In a small bowl, stir together the cocoa powder, food coloring, and vanilla. Add this mixture to the batter and beat on medium speed to combine well.
6. With the mixer running on low speed, add the buttermilk and flour in alternating batches, beating to combine after each addition. Turn the mixer to high speed and beat until smooth.
7. Add the vinegar, salt, and baking soda. Beat for 2 minutes more. Scoop the batter into the prepared muffin tin. Bake for 18 to 20 minutes until a toothpick inserted into the center of one of the cupcakes comes out clean.
8. Remove from the oven and let the cupcakes cool in the pan for several minutes before removing them from the tin to a wire rack to cool completely.

TO MAKE THE FROSTING

1. In a large bowl, with a handheld electric mixer or in a stand mixer fitted with a whisk attachment, whip the butter and cream cheese for about 5 minutes until smooth.
2. With the mixer running on low speed, slowly add the powdered sugar, beating until thoroughly incorporated.
3. Add the vanilla and whip the frosting on medium-high speed until fluffy and light.
4. When the cupcakes are cool, pipe, spread, or scoop the frosting onto them and serve at room temperature.

TRES LECHES CAKEDARK CHOCOLATE ICE CREAM

Serves 8

PREP TIME: 20 minutes

CHILLING AND FREEZING TIME: 5 hours

EQIPMENT: Freezer-safe storage container

Ingredients:

- 8 ounces semisweet chocolate, finely chopped
- 1 cup whole milk
- 2 cups heavy (whipping) cream
- ¾ cup granulated sugar
- Pinch salt
- 1 teaspoon vanilla extract

Directions:

1. In a medium microwave-safe bowl, combine the chocolate and milk. Microwave at 50 percent power, in 30-second intervals, stirring in between, until the chocolate melts and the mixture is smooth. Let cool for several minutes.
2. Meanwhile, in another medium bowl, combine the cream, sugar, and salt. Whisk, or use an electric mixer to beat, for about 3 minutes until the sugar dissolves.
3. Add the vanilla and the chocolate mixture and stir to combine well. Refrigerate for at least 2 hours until fully chilled.
4. Pour the mixture into a freezer-safe storage container, cover with plastic wrap, and freeze for about 45 minutes before checking on it the first time. As soon as it begins to freeze around the edges, mix it vigorously with a whisk, spatula, wooden spoon, or ideally, a handheld electric mixer or immersion blender. Continue to freeze, mixing it every 30 minutes, until it is fully frozen, about 3 hours total.
5. Keep frozen until ready to serve.

ROASTED STRAWBERRY ICE CREAM

Serves 8

PREP TIME: 15 minutes

COOK TIME: 35 to 40 minutes

CHILLING AND FREEZING TIME: 4 hours, 30 minutes

EQIPMENT: Freezer-safe storage container, a large baking dish with 2-inch sides

Ingredients:

- 1 pound fresh strawberries, cored and diced
- 3 tablespoons mild-flavored honey
- 1 cup whole milk
- ¾ cup sugar
- Pinch salt
- 2 cups heavy (whipping) cream
- 1 teaspoon vanilla extract

Directions:

1. Preheat the oven to 375°F.
2. Arrange the berries in a single layer in a large baking dish with 2-inch sides. Toss the berries with the honey. Roast for 35 to 40 minutes, stirring occasionally, until the juices have run out and thickened. Scrape the roasted fruit and all the juices into a bowl and refrigerate for at least 30 minutes.
3. In a medium bowl, combine the milk, sugar, and salt. Whisk, or use an electric mixer to beat, for about 3 minutes until the sugar dissolves.
4. Add the cream, vanilla, and roasted strawberries and stir to mix. Refrigerate for at least 1 hour until fully chilled.
5. Pour the mixture into a freezer-safe storage container, cover with plastic wrap, and freeze for about 45 minutes before checking on it the first time. As soon as it begins to freeze around the edges, mix it vigorously with a whisk, spatula, wooden spoon, or ideally, a handheld electric mixer or immersion blender. Continue to freeze, mixing it every 30 minutes, until it is fully frozen, about 3 hours total.
6. Keep frozen until ready to serve.

BUTTERSCOTCH ICE CREAM

Serves 8

PREP TIME: 20 minutes
COOK TIME: 5 minutes
CHILLING AND FREEZING TIME: 5 hours
EQIPMENT: Freezer-safe storage container
Ingredients:

- 1 cup packed light brown sugar
- 2 tablespoons unsalted butter
- 2 cups heavy (whipping) cream, divided
- 2 teaspoons vanilla extract
- 1 cup whole milk
- ¼ teaspoon kosher salt

Directions:

1. In a medium saucepan set over medium heat, combine the brown sugar and butter. Cook for about 5 minutes, stirring frequently with a silicone spatula, scraping the melted sugar from the bottom of the pan to prevent burning, until the butter and sugar are melted and smooth.
2. While whisking constantly, carefully add 1 cup of heavy cream, whisking for about 4 minutes until the mixture is smooth.
3. Remove the pan from the heat and stir in the vanilla.
4. In a medium bowl, combine the milk, salt, and remaining 1 cup of heavy cream. Whisk, or use an electric mixer to beat, for about 3 minutes until the sugar dissolves.
5. Add the butterscotch mixture and stir to mix well. Refrigerate for at least 2 hours, until fully chilled.
6. Pour the mixture into a freezer-safe storage container, cover with plastic wrap, and freeze for about 45 minutes before checking on it the first time. As soon as it begins to freeze around the edges, mix it vigorously with a whisk, spatula, wooden spoon, or ideally, a handheld electric mixer or immersion blender. Continue to freeze, mixing it every 30 minutes, until it is fully frozen, about 3 hours total.
7. Keep frozen until ready to serve.

ORANGE SHERBET

Serves 8

PREP TIME: 10 minutes
CHILLING AND FREEZING TIME: 5 hours
EQIPMENT: Freezer-safe storage container
Ingredients:

- ½ cup sugar
- ½ cup frozen orange juice concentrate, thawed or partially thawed
- 2 cups freshly squeezed orange juice
- 1½ cups whole milk

- 2 tablespoons freshly squeezed lemon juice
- 1 tablespoon vanilla extract
- ¼ teaspoon salt

Directions:

1. In a medium bowl, stir together the sugar, orange juice concentrate, orange juice, milk, lemon juice, vanilla, and salt until well combined and smooth. Refrigerate the mixture for at least 2 hours until fully chilled.
2. Pour the mixture into a freezer-safe storage container, cover with plastic wrap, and freeze for about 45 minutes before checking on it the first time. As soon as it begins to freeze around the edges, mix it vigorously with a whisk, spatula, wooden spoon, or ideally, a handheld electric mixer or immersion blender. Continue to freeze, mixing it every 30 minutes until it is fully frozen, about 3 hours total.
3. Store in the freezer until ready to serve.

CHOCOLATE CHIP COOKIES

Makes about 24 cookies

PREP TIME: 10 minutes
BAKE TIME: 9 to 11 minutes
EQIPMENT: Baking sheet

Ingredients:

- ½ cup (1 stick) unsalted butter, melted
- ½ cup granulated sugar
- ¼ cup packed light brown sugar
- 1 teaspoon vanilla extract
- 1 egg
- 1½ cups all-purpose flour
- ¾ teaspoon salt
- ½ teaspoon baking soda
- ¾ cup semisweet chocolate chips

Directions

1. Preheat the oven to 350°F.
2. In a large bowl, with a wooden spoon, electric mixer, or in the bowl of a stand mixer, cream together the butter, granulated sugar, and brown sugar until creamy.
3. Add the vanilla and egg. Mix just until incorporated.
4. Add the flour, salt, and baking soda. Mix until the mixture clumps.
5. Mix in the chocolate chips. Drop the batter by rounded tablespoons onto an ungreased baking sheet, leaving about 2 inches in between each cookie. Bake for 9 to 11 minutes until the cookies are pale golden brown.
6. Remove from the oven and let the cookies cool on the sheet for about 30 seconds. Transfer to a wire rack and let cool completely. Store at room temperature in an airtight container for several days.

ICED BROWN BUTTER OATMEAL COOKIES

Makes about 18 cookies

PREP TIME: 10 minutes
BAKE TIME: 10 to 12 minutes
EQIPMENT: Medium skillet, baking sheet
Ingredients:
FOR THE COOKIES

- 1 cup (2 sticks) unsalted butter
- 1 cup packed light brown sugar
- ½ cup granulated sugar
- 2 teaspoons vanilla extract
- 2 eggs, at room temperature
- 2 cups all-purpose flour
- 2 cups old-fashioned rolled oats
- 1 teaspoon baking soda
- 1 teaspoon ground cinnamon
- ¼ teaspoon salt

FOR THE ICING

- 1 cup powdered sugar
- 1 teaspoon vanilla extract
- 2 tablespoons low-fat or whole milk

Directions:
TO MAKE THE COOKIES

1. Preheat the oven to 350°F.
2. In a medium skillet set over medium heat, melt the butter and let it cook until it begins to foam, begins to brown, and smells toasty and nutty. Immediately remove the skillet from the heat and scrape the butter into a large bowl.
3. Add the brown sugar and granulated sugar. Using an electric mixer or wooden spoon, mix until well combined.
4. Add the vanilla and eggs, and beat until smooth.
5. Add the flour, oats, baking soda, cinnamon, and salt and beat until just combined. Drop the dough onto a baking sheet in heaping tablespoons, leaving about 2 inches between cookies. Bake for 10 to 12 minutes, until the cookies are golden brown around the edges.
6. Remove from the oven and let cool on the baking sheet for 2 to 3 minutes before transferring the cookies to a wire rack to cool completely. Store in an airtight container for up to 2 weeks.

TO MAKE THE ICING

1. In a medium bowl, stir together the powdered sugar, vanilla, and milk until smooth. Once the cookies have cooled for a few minutes, spoon the icing onto them, using about 2 teaspoons per cookie.

GINGER COOKIES

Makes about 24 cookies

PREP TIME: 10 minutes

BAKE TIME: 12 to 15 minutes

EQIPMENT: 2 baking sheets, medium bowl, large bowl

Ingredients:

- 1½ cups sugar, divided
- 2¼ cups all-purpose flour
- 2 teaspoons ground ginger
- 1 teaspoon ground cinnamon
- 1 teaspoon baking soda
- ½ teaspoon ground cloves
- ½ teaspoon salt
- ½ cup (1 stick) unsalted butter, at room temperature
- ⅓ cup molasses
- 1 egg

Directions:

1. Preheat the oven to 375°F.
2. Line 2 baking sheets with parchment paper, and put ½ cup of the sugar in a shallow bowl.
3. In a medium bowl, whisk the flour, ginger, cinnamon, baking soda, cloves, and salt.
4. In a large bowl, with a wooden spoon or electric mixer, cream together the butter and the remaining 1 cup of sugar.
5. Add the molasses and egg and continue to beat until the dough lightens. Add the dry ingredients and mix until thoroughly incorporated. With your hands, form the dough into 1-inch balls. Roll each ball in the bowl of sugar to coat lightly. Arrange the dough balls 2 inches apart on the prepared sheets. Bake for 12 to 15 minutes until the cookies are cracked and golden brown.
6. Remove from the oven and let the cookies cool on the baking sheet for 5 minutes before transferring them to a wire rack to cool completely. Store in an airtight container for up to 2 weeks.

CHOCOLATE–PEANUT BUTTER COOKIES

Makes about 50 cookies

PREP TIME: 10 minutes

SETTING TIME: 30 minutes

EQIPMENT: Baking sheet, medium saucepan

Ingredients:

- 2 cups sugar
- ½ cup low-fat or whole milk
- ½ cup (1 stick) unsalted butter

- ¼ cup unsweetened cocoa powder
- 3 cups old-fashioned rolled oats
- 1 cup smooth peanut butter
- 1 tablespoon vanilla extract
- ¼ teaspoon salt

Directions:

1. Line a baking sheet with parchment paper.
2. In a medium saucepan set over medium heat, combine the sugar, milk, butter, and cocoa powder. Bring to a boil, stirring occasionally. Let the mixture boil for 1 minute and remove the pan from the heat.
3. Stir in the oats, peanut butter, vanilla, and salt until combined. Using a tablespoon, drop rounds of dough onto the prepared sheet. Let sit at room temperature until the mixture cools and hardens, about 30 minutes. Serve immediately or refrigerate in an airtight container for up to 1 week.

PEANUT BUTTER COOKIES

Makes about 18 cookies

PREP TIME: 10 minutes
COOK TIME: 12 minutes
EQIPMENT: Baking sheet
Ingredients:

- 1 cup sugar
- 1 cup peanut butter
- 1 egg

Directions:

1. Preheat the oven to 350°F.
2. In a medium bowl, stir together the sugar, peanut butter, and egg until well combined. Scoop heaping tablespoons of dough onto an ungreased baking sheet. Using the tines of a fork, press down on each dough mound to flatten it and make a pattern on top. Turn the fork 90 degrees and press down again to form a crisscross pattern.
3. Bake for 12 minutes.
4. Remove from the oven and let cool on the baking sheet for about 2 minutes before transferring to a wire rack to cool completely. Store at room temperature in an airtight container for several days.

MAPLE PECAN DROP COOKIES

Makes about 50 cookies

PREP TIME: 10 minutes
SETTING TIME: 30 minutes
EQIPMENT: 2 baking sheets, medium saucepan, blender or food processor
Ingredients:

- Nonstick baking spray
- ½ cup unsalted butter, melted

- ½ cup pure maple syrup
- ¼ cup packed light brown sugar
- ½ teaspoon vanilla extract
- ¼ teaspoon salt
- 1 cup old-fashioned rolled oats, toasted
- 1 cup finely chopped pecans, toasted

Directions:

1. Line 2 baking sheets with parchment paper and mist with baking spray.
2. In a medium saucepan set over medium-high heat, combine the butter, maple syrup, and brown sugar. Bring to a boil. Cook for 3 minutes, stirring. Remove the pan from the heat and immediately stir in the vanilla and salt. Let cool for 3 minutes.
3. Put the oats in a blender or food processor and grind coarsely.
4. Add the ground oats and pecans to the butter mixture and stir to mix well. Using a tablespoon, drop rounds of dough onto the prepared sheets. Let sit at room temperature for 30 minutes to cool and harden. Serve immediately or store in an airtight container, separated by sheets of parchment, for up to 1 week.

WHITE CHOCOLATE CRISP COOKIES

Makes about 50 cookies

PREP TIME: 10 minutes

CHILLING TIME: 30 minutes

EQIPMENT: 2 baking sheets, microwave or double boiler

Ingredients:

- 2 cups crisped rice cereal
- 1 cup mini marshmallows
- ½ cup creamy peanut butter
- 1 pound chopped white chocolate, or white chocolate chips

Directions:

1. Line 2 baking sheets with parchment paper.
2. In a large bowl, stir together the cereal and marshmallows.
3. In a large microwave-safe bowl, combine the peanut butter and white chocolate. Microwave at 50 percent power, in 30-second intervals, stirring in between, until completely melted and smooth. Pour the mixture over the cereal and marshmallows and stir to coat completely.
4. Using a tablespoon, drop the mixture on the prepared sheets. Refrigerate until the chocolate sets, about 30 minutes. Serve immediately or refrigerate in an airtight container, separated by sheets of parchment, for up to 1 week.

VANILLA ICE CREAM

Serves 8

PREP TIME: 10 minutes

CHILLING AND FREEZING TIME: 4 hours

EQIPMENT: Freezer-safe storage container

Ingredients:

- 1 cup whole milk
- ¾ cup granulated sugar
- Pinch salt
- 2 cups heavy (whipping) cream
- 1 tablespoon vanilla extract

Directions:

1. In a medium bowl, combine the milk, sugar, and salt. Whisk, or use an electric mixer to beat, for about 3 minutes until the sugar dissolves.

2. Add the cream and vanilla and stir to mix. Refrigerate for at least 1 hour.

3. Pour the mixture into a freezer-safe storage container, cover with plastic wrap, and freeze for about 45 minutes before checking on it the first time. As soon as it begins to freeze around the edges, mix it vigorously with a whisk, spatula, wooden spoon, or ideally, a handheld electric mixer or immersion blender. Continue to freeze, mixing it every 30 minutes, until it is fully frozen, about 3 hours total.

4. Keep frozen until ready to serve.

DARK CHOCOLATE ICE CREAM

Serves 8

PREP TIME: 20 minutes

CHILLING AND FREEZING TIME: 5 hours

EQIPMENT: Freezer-safe storage container

Ingredients:

- 8 ounces semisweet chocolate, finely chopped
- 1 cup whole milk
- 2 cups heavy (whipping) cream
- ¾ cup granulated sugar
- Pinch salt
- 1 teaspoon vanilla extract

Directions:

6. In a medium microwave-safe bowl, combine the chocolate and milk. Microwave at 50 percent power, in 30-second intervals, stirring in between, until the chocolate melts and the mixture is smooth. Let cool for several minutes.

7. Meanwhile, in another medium bowl, combine the cream, sugar, and salt. Whisk, or use an electric mixer to beat, for about 3 minutes until the sugar dissolves.

8. Add the vanilla and the chocolate mixture and stir to combine well. Refrigerate for at least 2 hours until fully chilled.

9. Pour the mixture into a freezer-safe storage container, cover with plastic wrap, and freeze for about 45 minutes before checking on it the first time. As soon as it begins to freeze around the edges, mix it vigorously with a whisk, spatula, wooden spoon, or ideally, a handheld electric mixer or immersion blender. Continue to freeze, mixing it every 30 minutes, until it is fully frozen, about 3 hours total.

10. Keep frozen until ready to serve.

ROASTED STRAWBERRY ICE CREAM

Serves 8

PREP TIME: 15 minutes

COOK TIME: 35 to 40 minutes

CHILLING AND FREEZING TIME: 4 hours, 30 minutes

EQIPMENT: Freezer-safe storage container, a large baking dish with 2-inch sides

Ingredients:

- 1 pound fresh strawberries, cored and diced
- 3 tablespoons mild-flavored honey
- 1 cup whole milk
- ¾ cup sugar
- Pinch salt
- 2 cups heavy (whipping) cream
- 1 teaspoon vanilla extract

Directions:

7. Preheat the oven to 375°F.

8. Arrange the berries in a single layer in a large baking dish with 2-inch sides. Toss the berries with the honey. Roast for 35 to 40 minutes, stirring occasionally, until the juices have run out and thickened. Scrape the roasted fruit and all the juices into a bowl and refrigerate for at least 30 minutes.

9. In a medium bowl, combine the milk, sugar, and salt. Whisk, or use an electric mixer to beat, for about 3 minutes until the sugar dissolves.

10. Add the cream, vanilla, and roasted strawberries and stir to mix. Refrigerate for at least 1 hour until fully chilled.

11. Pour the mixture into a freezer-safe storage container, cover with plastic wrap, and freeze for about 45 minutes before checking on it the first time. As soon as it begins to freeze around the edges, mix it vigorously with a whisk, spatula, wooden spoon, or ideally, a handheld electric mixer or immersion blender. Continue to freeze, mixing it every 30 minutes, until it is fully frozen, about 3 hours total.

12. Keep frozen until ready to serve.

BUTTERSCOTCH
ICE CREAM

Serves 8

PREP TIME: 20 minutes

COOK TIME: 5 minutes

CHILLING AND FREEZING TIME: 5 hours

EQIPMENT: Freezer-safe storage container

Ingredients:

- 1 cup packed light brown sugar
- 2 tablespoons unsalted butter
- 2 cups heavy (whipping) cream, divided

- 2 teaspoons vanilla extract
- 1 cup whole milk
- ¼ teaspoon kosher salt

Directions:

8. In a medium saucepan set over medium heat, combine the brown sugar and butter. Cook for about 5 minutes, stirring frequently with a silicone spatula, scraping the melted sugar from the bottom of the pan to prevent burning, until the butter and sugar are melted and smooth.

9. While whisking constantly, carefully add 1 cup of heavy cream, whisking for about 4 minutes until the mixture is smooth.

10. Remove the pan from the heat and stir in the vanilla.

11. In a medium bowl, combine the milk, salt, and remaining 1 cup of heavy cream. Whisk, or use an electric mixer to beat, for about 3 minutes until the sugar dissolves.

12. Add the butterscotch mixture and stir to mix well. Refrigerate for at least 2 hours, until fully chilled.

13. Pour the mixture into a freezer-safe storage container, cover with plastic wrap, and freeze for about 45 minutes before checking on it the first time. As soon as it begins to freeze around the edges, mix it vigorously with a whisk, spatula, wooden spoon, or ideally, a handheld electric mixer or immersion blender. Continue to freeze, mixing it every 30 minutes, until it is fully frozen, about 3 hours total.

14. Keep frozen until ready to serve.

DARK CHOCOLATE TRUFFLES

Makes about 30 truffles

PREP TIME: 30 minutes
CHILLING TIME: 2 hours
EQIPMENT: Baking sheet

Ingredients:

- 12 ounces dark chocolate, chopped
- 3 tablespoons unsalted butter
- ⅓ cup heavy (whipping) cream
- 1 teaspoon vanilla extract
- Coatings as desired, such as sweetened or unsweetened cocoa powder, decorating sugars, colored sprinkles, finely chopped nuts, or shredded coconut

Directions:

6. In a large microwave-safe bowl, combine the dark chocolate, butter, and cream. Microwave at 50 percent power, in 30-second intervals, stirring in between, until the chocolate is fully melted and the mixture is smooth.

7. Whisk in the vanilla. Let the mixture cool to room temperature, cover with plastic wrap, and refrigerate for 2 hours.

8. Line the baking sheet with parchment paper.

9. With a small cookie scoop or a melon baller, scoop out balls of the chocolate. Gently roll the balls between your hands to smooth the edges. Place each ball on the prepared baking sheet once it is formed. Repeat until all the chocolate mixture has been used. You should get around 30 balls.

10. Place your desired coating(s) into shallow dishes and roll the balls in them to coat well. Return the coated balls to the baking sheet. Once all the balls are coated, refrigerate until ready to serve.

DARK CHOCOLATE SORBET

Serves 8

PREP TIME: 15 minutes

CHILLING AND FREEZING TIME: 5 to 6 hours

EQIPMENT: Freezer-safe storage container

Ingredients:

- 1 cup sugar
- ¾ cup unsweetened Dutch process cocoa powder
- Pinch salt
- 6 ounces semisweet chocolate, finely chopped
- 1 teaspoon vanilla extract

Directions:

5. In a large saucepan over medium-high heat, whisk the sugar, cocoa powder, salt, and 1¼ cups water. Bring to a boil and let it cook for about 45 seconds, whisking constantly. Remove from the heat and immediately add the chocolate. Stir until the chocolate completely melts and the mixture is smooth.

6. Stir in the vanilla and 1 cup water. Refrigerate for at least 2 hours until fully chilled.

7. Pour the mixture into a freezer-safe storage container, cover with plastic wrap, and freeze for about 45 minutes before checking on it the first time. As soon as it begins to freeze around the edges, mix it vigorously with a whisk, spatula, wooden spoon, or ideally, a handheld electric mixer or immersion blender. Continue to freeze, mixing it every 30 minutes, until it is fully frozen, 3 to 4 hours total.

8. Keep frozen until ready to serve.

LEMON SORBET

Serves 8

PREP TIME: 20 minutes

CHILLING AND FREEZING TIME: 5 to 6 hours

EQIPMENT: Freezer-safe storage container

Ingredients:

- 2 cups light corn syrup
- 1½ cups cold water
- 1 cup freshly squeezed lemon juice (from about 6 lemons)
- 1 tablespoon vodka
- Zest of 1 lemon
- ½ teaspoon salt

Directions:

4. In a medium bowl, whisk the corn syrup, water, lemon juice, vodka, lemon zest, and salt until smooth and well combined. Refrigerate for at least 2 hours until fully chilled.

5. Pour the mixture into a freezer-safe storage container, cover with plastic wrap, and freeze for about 45 minutes before checking on it the first time. As soon as it begins to freeze around the edges, mix it vigorously with a whisk, spatula, wooden spoon, or ideally, a handheld electric mixer or immersion blender. Continue to freeze, mixing it every 30 minutes, until it is fully frozen, 3 to 4 hours total.

6. Keep frozen until ready to serve.

TROPICAL ICE POPS

Makes 10 ice pops

PREP TIME: 5 minutes

FREEZING TIME: 6 hours

EQIPMENT: Blender, 10 ice pop molds or small paper cups and ice pop sticks

Ingredients:

- 4 cups frozen pineapple
- 1 cup canned coconut milk
- 2 teaspoons vanilla extract
- 2 tablespoons sugar, as needed

Directions:

3. In a blender, purée the pineapple, coconut milk, and vanilla until smooth. Taste and add sugar as needed, blending to incorporate it.

4. Pour the mixture into 10 ice pop molds or paper cups and freeze for about 45 minutes before adding the sticks. Freeze for at least 6 hours until frozen solid. Keep frozen.

WATERMELON ICE POPS

Makes 10 ice pops

PREP TIME: 20 minutes

FREEZING TIME: 7 hours

EQIPMENT: Blender, 10 ice pop molds or small paper cups and ice pop sticks

Ingredients:

- 3½ cups cubed seedless watermelon
- 5 tablespoons sugar, divided
- 1 tablespoon freshly squeezed lemon juice
- 1 tablespoon mini chocolate chips
- 10 kiwi fruits, peeled and diced

Directions:

5. In a blender, combine the watermelon with 2 tablespoons of sugar and the lemon juice and blend until smooth. Pour the mixture into 10 ice pop molds, filling the molds two-thirds full.

6. Add a few chocolate chips to each mold, pressing them down into the juice with one of the ice pop sticks or a skewer. Freeze for at least 4 hours.

7. Meanwhile, in a blender, combine the kiwi with the remaining 3 tablespoons of sugar and blend until smooth. Strain the mixture through a fine-mesh sieve to remove the seeds. Chill for at least 30 minutes.

8. Once the watermelon layer is frozen, remove the molds from the freezer and top off each mold with 2 tablespoons of kiwi mixture and insert the sticks. Return to the freezer and freeze for at least 3 hours more until solid.

ESPRESSO FROZEN YOGURT POPS

Makes 10 frozen yogurt pops

PREP TIME: 5 minutes

FREEZING TIME: 6 hours, 45 minutes

EQIPMENT: 10 ice pop molds or small paper cups and ice pop sticks

Ingredients:

- 3 cups vanilla yogurt
- ⅔ cup low-fat or whole milk
- ½ cup sugar
- 2 tablespoons instant espresso powder

Directions:

3. In a large pitcher, stir together the yogurt, milk, sugar, and espresso powder until well combined. Pour the mixture into 10 ice pop molds.

4. Freeze for at least 45 minutes before inserting the sticks. Freeze for at least 6 hours until frozen solid. Keep frozen until ready to serve

BLACKBERRY FROZEN YOGURT SWIRL POPS

Makes 10 frozen yogurt pops

PREP TIME: 10 minutes

COOK TIME: 10 minutes

CHILLING AND FREEZING TIME: 6 hours, 30 minutes

EQIPMENT: Medium saucepan, blender, 10 ice pop molds or small paper cups and ice pop sticks

Ingredients:

- 2 cups fresh blackberries, halved if large
- 1 tablespoon freshly squeezed lemon juice
- ½ cup plus 2 tablespoons sugar, divided
- 1½ cups plain yogurt

Directions:

6. In a medium bowl, toss the berries with the lemon juice and 2 tablespoons of sugar. Set aside.

7. In a medium saucepan set over medium-high heat, combine ½ cup water with the remaining ½ cup of sugar and cook, stirring, until the water boils and the sugar dissolves. Lower the heat and simmer for 5 minutes more until the mixture is syrupy. Remove from the heat and transfer to a storage container or pitcher. Refrigerate for about 30 minutes until chilled.

8. In another medium bowl, whisk the yogurt with the chilled syrup.

9. In a blender, purée the berries until mostly smooth. Strain through a fine-mesh sieve into a bowl to remove the seeds.

10. To make the ice pops, fill the molds with alternating layers of yogurt mixture and berry purée until the molds are full. Leave about ½ inch at the top to allow for expansion as they freeze. Use an ice pop stick, skewer, or chopstick to gently swirl together the two mixtures. Transfer the pops to the freezer for about 45 minutes before inserting the sticks. Continue to freeze for at least 6 hours until frozen. Keep frozen until ready to serve.

WITH CHOCOLATE COOKIES

Makes 12 ice cream sandwiches

PREP TIME: 30 minutes

COOK TIME: 10 to 12 minutes

CHILLING AND FREEZING TIME: 1 hour, 30 minutes

EQIPMENT: 9-by-13-inch baking pan, electric mixer

Ingredients:

- ½ gallon vanilla ice cream, slightly softened
- 2 ⅔ cups all-purpose flour, plus more for the work surface
- ⅔ cup plus ¼ cup unsweetened cocoa powder
- ¾ teaspoon salt
- 1¼ cups (2½ sticks) unsalted butter
- 1 cup sugar
- 2 egg yolks
- 2 teaspoons vanilla extract

Directions:

12. Line a 9-by-13-inch baking pan with parchment paper (use enough paper so it hangs over the sides). Transfer the softened ice cream to the prepared pan and use a rubber spatula to spread it into an even layer. Cover with plastic wrap and freeze for at least 1 hour until frozen solid.

13. Preheat the oven to 350°F.

14. Line 2 baking sheets with parchment paper.

15. Meanwhile, in a medium bowl sift together the flour, cocoa powder, and salt.

16. In a large bowl, using a handheld electric mixer or a stand mixer at medium speed, cream together the butter and sugar for about 1 minute until creamy and lightened in color.

17. Add the egg yolks and vanilla and mix to incorporate.

18. Add the dry ingredients and mix until just combined. Split the dough into 2 equal pieces and pat each piece into a 5-inch square. Wrap the squares in plastic wrap and refrigerate for 30 minutes.

19. When the dough is thoroughly chilled, turn it out onto a lightly floured surface and roll each square into an 8-by-12-inch rectangle. Cut each rectangle into 6 (2-by-8-inch) strips. Halve each strip widthwise to make 24 (2-by-4-inch) rectangles. Transfer the cookies to the prepared sheets, and using a skewer or chopstick, make 2 lines of holes running down the length of each cookie. Bake for 10 to 12 minutes until firm.

20. Remove from the oven and transfer the cookies to a wire rack to cool completely.

21. When the cookies are completely cooled, lift the ice cream out of the baking pan using the parchment paper. Trim the edges so they are straight, creating a straight-sided 8-by-12-inch rectangle. Cut the ice cream into 6 (2-by-8-inch) strips and halve each strip widthwise to make 12 (2-by-4-inch) rectangles.

22. Place each ice cream rectangle between 2 cookies and press together slightly. Serve immediately or wrap in parchment paper or plastic wrap and freeze.

CHOCOLATE-HAZELNUT FUDGE POPS

Makes 6 ice pops

PREP TIME: 10 minutes

FREEZING TIME: 6 hours

EQIPMENT: Medium saucepan, 6 ice pop molds or small paper cups and ice pop sticks

Ingredients:

- 1 cup whole milk
- 1 cup chocolate-hazelnut spread (like Nutella)
- ½ cup heavy (whipping) cream
- 2 tablespoons dark cocoa powder
- 1 teaspoon vanilla extract

Directions:

3. In a medium saucepan set over low heat, stir together the milk, chocolate-hazelnut spread, cream, cocoa powder, and vanilla for 5 to 10 minutes until the chocolate-hazelnut spread is fully melted and the mixture is well combined. Remove from the heat and set aside to cool for about 10 minutes.

4. Pour the chocolate mixture into 6 ice pop molds or paper cups set on a sheet pan. Freeze for about 45 minutes before adding the sticks. Continue to freeze for at least 6 hours until completely frozen solid. Keep frozen until ready to serve.

TIRAMISU ICE CREAM CAKE

Serves 8

PREP TIME: 30 minutes

FREEZING TIME: 6 hours, 30 minutes

EQIPMENT: 9-inch springform pan

Ingredients:

- Nonstick baking spray, for preparing the pan
- 25 chocolate wafer cookies, finely crushed, plus more for garnish (I prefer Nabisco Famous Chocolate Wafers)
- 2 tablespoons unsalted butter, melted
- 3 pints coffee ice cream, divided
- 1½ cups brewed espresso or strong coffee, cooled
- 30 soft ladyfingers, divided
- 1 cup heavy (whipping) cream
- 2 tablespoons sugar
- ¼ cup finely grated semisweet chocolate, or cocoa powder

Directions:

8. Coat the inside of a 9-inch springform pan with nonstick baking spray.

9. In a small bowl, stir together the cookie crumbs and butter. Press the mixture into the bottom of the prepared pan. Transfer the pan to the freezer.

10. Let the ice cream sit on the countertop at room temperature for about 15 minutes until it softens. Transfer to a large bowl and stir it until it softens into a spreadable consistency.

11. Remove the pan from the freezer and spread ⅓ of the ice cream over the crust. Dip the ladyfingers into the coffee and arrange them in a single layer covering the layer of ice cream. Repeat twice more so you

have 3 layers of ice cream separated by 3 layers of espresso-dipped ladyfingers. Cover with plastic wrap and return to the freezer for about 30 minutes.

12. In a large bowl, combine the cream and sugar, using a handheld electric mixer or a stand mixer to whip the ingredients until the cream holds soft peaks.

13. Remove the pan from the freezer again and spread the whipped cream over the top. Garnish with the shaved chocolate or cocoa powder, cover with plastic wrap, and return the pan to the freezer for at least 6 hours.

14. To serve, unmold the cake from the springform pan and slice it into wedges. Serve straight out of the freezer and keep any unused portion covered and frozen.

STRAWBERRY SHORTCAKE

Serves 6

PREP TIME: 20 minutes

COOK TIME: 18 to 20 minutes

CHILLING AND COOLING TIME: 45 minutes

EQIPMENT: 8-inch square baking pan, electric mixer

Ingredients:

- 1½ pounds fresh strawberries, stemmed and quartered
- ½ cup sugar, divided
- 2 cups all-purpose flour
- 2 teaspoons baking powder
- ¾ teaspoon salt
- ¼ teaspoon baking soda
- 3 cups chilled heavy (whipping) cream, divided
- 1½ teaspoons vanilla extract

Directions:

9. In a large bowl, toss the strawberries with 3 tablespoons of sugar. Refrigerate for at least 30 minutes to let the strawberries macerate.

10. Preheat the oven to 400°F.

11. In a medium bowl, stir together the flour, baking powder, baking soda, salt, and 2 tablespoons of sugar.

12. Add 1½ cups of cream and stir until just combined. Transfer the batter to an 8-inch square baking pan and bake for 18 to 20 minutes until golden brown.

13. Remove from the oven and invert the cake onto a wire rack to cool.

14. While the cake cools, make the whipped cream. Using a handheld electric mixer or a stand mixer, beat the remaining 1½ cups of cream with the remaining 3 tablespoons of sugar for about 3 minutes until the cream holds soft peaks.

15. Add the vanilla and beat to incorporate.

16. Once cooled, cut the cake into 6 rectangular pieces and split each horizontally. Put the bottom halves of the cake onto 6 serving plates and spoon some of the strawberries, along with the juice that has collected in the bowl, over them. Add a generous dollop of whipped cream and top with the cake tops. Serve immediately.

ESPRESSO ICEBOX CAKE

Serves 8

PREP TIME: 20 minutes

CHILLING AND FREEZING TIME: 9 hours

EQIPMENT: 10-inch springform pan, electric mixer

Ingredients:

- 3 cups chilled heavy (whipping) cream, divided
- ½ cup plus 1 tablespoon sugar, divided
- 1 cup (about 9 ounces) mascarpone cheese, at room temperature
- ¼ cup coffee liqueur, such as Kahlua
- 42 chocolate wafer cookies, divided (I prefer Nabisco Famous Chocolate Wafers)
- 1 tablespoon instant espresso powder

Directions:

7. In a large bowl, using a handheld electric mixer or in a stand mixer, beat together 2 cups of cream with 6 tablespoons of sugar for about 3 minutes until the cream holds soft peaks.
8. With the mixer set on low speed, add the mascarpone and coffee liqueur. Mix to combine.
9. Spread 1¼ cups of the mascarpone mixture over the bottom of the springform pan in an even layer. Top with 14 chocolate wafers, slightly overlapping them as needed. Top the wafers with another 1¼ cups of mascarpone and another layer of 14 wafers. Top with the remaining mascarpone, smoothing the top with a spatula. Cover the pan and freeze for about 1 hour until the cake is firm. Transfer the cake to the refrigerator and chill for 8 hours or longer until the cookies are soft and the cake is set.
10. Crush the remaining wafers in a blender, food processor, or in a resealable plastic bag with a rolling pin.
11. In a medium bowl, using an electric mixer or a stand mixer set at medium speed, whip the remaining 1 cup of cream with the espresso powder and the remaining 3 tablespoons of sugar for about 3 minutes, just until the cream holds stiff peaks.
12. Unmold the cake from the pan, spread the espresso cream over the top and sides, and sprinkle the wafer crumbs over the top. Serve chilled.

CINNAMON CUSTARD

Serves 4

PREP TIME: 5 minutes

COOK TIME: 10 minutes

EQIPMENT: Medium saucepan, fine-mesh sieve

Ingredients:

- ½ cup sugar
- 2 (3-inch) cinnamon sticks, broken
- 1 cup low-fat or whole milk
- 1 cup heavy (whipping) cream
- 6 egg yolks, at room temperature
- 1 tablespoon cornstarch

- Ground cinnamon, for garnish

Directions:

1. Spread the sugar over the bottom of a medium saucepan set over medium heat. Add the cinnamon sticks and cook for about 5 minutes just until the sugar melts and turns golden.

2. Carefully pour in the milk and cream, being careful not to splatter, and bring the mixture to a boil.

3. In a large bowl, whisk the egg yolks and cornstarch. While whisking continuously, slowly add the hot milk mixture to the yolks. Return the mixture to the saucepan and place it over medium heat. Cook for about 5 minutes, stirring, until it thickens.

4. Strain the thickened mixture through a fine-mesh sieve into a serving bowl, discarding the cinnamon sticks. Garnish with a bit of ground cinnamon and serve warm. Cover any leftovers with plastic wrap and refrigerate for up to 3 days.

PLUM CUSTARD

Serves 6

PREP TIME: 10 minutes

COOK TIME: 45 minutes to 1 hour

EQIPMENT: 9-inch pie dish, fine-mesh sieve

Ingredients:

- Unsalted butter, for preparing the pan
- 1¼ cups low-fat or whole milk
- ⅓ cup sugar
- 2 eggs
- ½ cup all-purpose flour
- 1 tablespoon vanilla extract
- ⅛ teaspoon salt
- 4 plums, pitted and quartered
- Powdered sugar, for garnish

Directions:

7. Preheat the oven to 350°F.

8. Generously grease a 9-inch pie dish with butter.

9. In a medium bowl, whisk the milk, sugar, eggs, flour, vanilla, and salt. Strain the mixture through a fine-mesh sieve into the prepared pie dish.

10. Arrange the plum wedges on top of the batter.

11. Bake for 45 minutes to 1 hour until the cake is puffed, golden brown, and a toothpick inserted into the center comes out clean.

12. Garnish with powdered sugar, slice, and serve warm or at room temperature. Cover any leftovers with plastic wrap and refrigerate for up to 3 days.

ARBORIO RICE PUDDING

Serves 4 to 6

PREP TIME: 15 minutes (including 10 minutes to soak the rice)

COOK TIME: 1 hour

EQIPMENT: Medium saucepan, 8-inch square baking dish

Ingredients:

- 2 tablespoons unsalted butter, plus more for preparing the baking dish
- 1 cup uncooked arborio rice
- 2 cups whole milk
- ½ cup heavy (whipping) cream
- Pinch salt
- ¼ cup sugar
- 1 teaspoon vanilla extract
- ½ teaspoon ground cinnamon

Directions:

8. Preheat the oven to 325°F.
9. Generously grease an 8-inch square baking dish with butter.
10. In a medium saucepan, combine the rice, milk, cream, and salt. Let the rice soak for 10 minutes.
11. Place the saucepan over medium-high heat and bring just to a boil. Remove the saucepan from the heat and pour the rice mixture into the prepared dish.
12. Stir in the butter, sugar, and vanilla.
13. Sprinkle the cinnamon over the top. Bake for about 1 hour, until the rice is tender, all the liquid has been soaked up, and the top is golden brown.
14. Remove from the oven and serve warm. Cover any leftovers with plastic wrap and refrigerate for up to 3 days.

DARK CHOCOLATE PUDDING

Serves 4

PREP TIME: 5 minutes
COOK TIME: 4 minutes
EQIPMENT: Medium saucepan

Ingredients:

- ¼ cup cornstarch
- 3 tablespoons unsweetened cocoa powder
- ⅓ cup sugar
- ¼ teaspoon salt
- 3 cups whole milk
- 4 ounces dark chocolate, melted in the microwave (see tip)
- 2 teaspoons vanilla extract

Directions:

4. In a large saucepan, whisk the cornstarch, cocoa powder, sugar, and salt.
5. Add the milk and whisk until well combined. Place the saucepan over medium heat and bring to a simmer. Cook for about 4 minutes, whisking continuously, until the mixture thickens. Transfer the hot mixture to a medium bowl.
6. Whisk in the melted chocolate and vanilla. Serve immediately or cover with plastic wrap and refrigerate

for up to 3 days.

MANGO PUDDING

Serves 8

PREP TIME: 5 minutes
COOK TIME: 10 minutes
CHILLING TIME: 2 hours
EQIPMENT: 8 (6-ounce) ramekins, small saucepan, blender or food processor, fine-mesh sieve
Ingredients:

- 1¼ cups sugar, divided
- 2½ cups cold water, divided
- 1 pound frozen mango chunks
- 2 (¼-ounce) packets unflavored gelatin
- ½ teaspoon salt
- 1 cup heavy (whipping) cream, chilled
- 1 teaspoon freshly squeezed lime juice

Directions:

8. Arrange 8 (6-ounce) ramekins on a baking sheet.
9. In a small saucepan set over medium-high heat, combine ½ cup of sugar with ¾ cup of cold water and heat for about 4 minutes, stirring, until the sugar fully dissolves and the mixture comes to a boil.
10. In a blender or food processor, combine the frozen mango and sugar mixture. Process until smooth. Strain the mixture through a fine-mesh sieve into a medium bowl, discarding any solids.
11. In a small saucepan set over high heat, bring 1¼ cups water to a boil.
12. In a large bowl, whisk the remaining ¾ cup of sugar with the gelatin and salt.
13. Whisk in the remaining ½ cup of cold water and continue to whisk for about 30 seconds. Add the boiling water and continue to whisk for about 1 minute until the sugar and gelatin completely dissolve.
14. Stir in 2 cups of mango purée along with the heavy cream and lime juice, mixing until well combined. Spoon the mixture into the ramekins, dividing evenly. Refrigerate for at least 2 hours until firm. Serve chilled. Cover any leftovers with plastic wrap and refrigerate for up to 3 days.

LEMON PUDDING CAKE

Serves 6 to 8

PREP TIME: 15 minutes
COOK TIME: 45 minutes to 1 hour
EQIPMENT: 8-inch square or round cake pan, whisk, electric mixer
Ingredients:

- ½ cup (1 stick) unsalted butter, melted, plus more for preparing the baking dish
- 4 eggs, at room temperature, separated
- ¾ cup sugar
- 1 teaspoon vanilla extract
- ¾ cup all-purpose flour

- Zest of 1 lemon
- ¼ cup freshly squeezed lemon juice
- 1¾ cups low-fat or whole milk, slightly warmed
- Powdered sugar, for dusting

Directions:

12. Preheat the oven to 325°F.
13. Grease an 8-inch cake pan with butter.
14. In a large bowl, using an electric mixer, whip the egg whites until stiff peaks form.
15. In another large bowl, whisk the egg yolks and sugar until the mixture lightens.
16. Add the melted butter and vanilla and beat for 1 to 2 minutes more.
17. Add the flour and mix until it is fully incorporated.
18. Whisk in the lemon zest and juice.
19. While whisking or beating continuously, add the milk.
20. Gently fold in the egg whites, about ⅓ at a time, until they are mostly incorporated but bits of white are still visible. Transfer the batter to the prepared pan and bake for 45 minutes to 1 hour until the top is firm to the touch.
21. Remove from the oven and let the cake cool completely.
22. Dust the top with powdered sugar, and serve at room temperature. Cover any leftovers with plastic wrap and refrigerate for up to 3 days.

CHOCOLATE BROWNIE PUDDING CAKE

Serves 6 to 8

PREP TIME: 15 minutes
COOK TIME: 1 hour
EQIPMENT: 8-inch square or round cake pan, whisk, electric mixer

Ingredients:

- ½ cup (1 stick) unsalted butter, melted, plus more for preparing the pan
- ¼ cup plus 3 tablespoons all-purpose flour, plus more for preparing the pan
- 4 eggs, at room temperature, separated
- 1 tablespoon water
- 1 teaspoon vanilla extract
- Pinch salt
- ¼ cup plus 2 tablespoons unsweetened cocoa powder
- 2 cups low-fat or whole milk, slightly warmed
- 1 teaspoon vinegar
- ¾ cup powdered sugar

Directions:

10. Preheat the oven to 325°F.
11. Grease an 8-inch cake pan with butter and dust with flour.
12. In a large bowl, whisk the egg yolks with the water until the eggs become creamy and light.
13. Add the melted butter, vanilla, and salt and beat until the mixture is light and fluffy.

14. Add the flour and cocoa powder in 3 batches, mixing after each addition until thoroughly incorporated.

15. Add the milk, a little at a time, mixing thoroughly after each addition.

16. In another large bowl, with a handheld mixer or whisk, whip the egg whites and vinegar until stiff peaks form. Add a scoop of the whipped egg whites to the chocolate mixture and gently fold it in.

17. Add a scoop of the chocolate mixture to the egg whites and gently fold to combine. Continue adding the chocolate mixture a little at a time to the egg white mixture, gently folding it in. Transfer the batter to the prepared pan and bake for about 1 hour until the cake is mostly set, but still slightly jiggly in the center.

18. Remove from the oven and set the pan on a wire rack to cool completely before slicing and serving. Cover any leftovers with plastic wrap and refrigerate for up to 3 days.

VANILLA BEAN POTS DE CRÈME

Serves 8

PREP TIME: 15 minutes

COOK TIME: 25 to 30 minutes

CHILLING TIME: 4 hours

EQIPMENT: Medium saucepan, whisk, large baking dish, 8 (4-ounce) ramekins, fine-mesh sieve

Ingredients:

- 2 cups heavy (whipping) cream
- ½ cup whole milk
- ¼ teaspoon salt
- 1 vanilla bean, split lengthwise
- 6 egg yolks
- ¼ cup sugar
- Lightly sweetened whipped cream, for serving (optional)

Directions:

8. Preheat the oven to 300°F.

9. Place 8 (4-ounce) ramekins in a large baking dish.

10. In a medium saucepan set over medium heat, whisk the cream, milk, and salt.

11. Scrape the seeds from the inside of the vanilla bean into the cream, and then add the pod. Heat for about 4 minutes, stirring occasionally, until the mixture simmers.

12. Meanwhile, in a large bowl, whisk the egg yolks and sugar for about 4 minutes until the mixture becomes pale. While whisking continuously, add the hot cream mixture to the yolk mixture in a thin, slow stream. Continue whisking until the mixture is smooth. Strain it through a fine-mesh sieve into a large bowl or pitcher.

13. Ladle or pour the mixture into the ramekins, dividing evenly. Add enough hot water to the baking dish so it comes about halfway up the sides of the ramekins. Carefully transfer the baking dish to the oven and bake for 25 to 30 minutes until set around the edges, but still jiggly in the center.

14. Remove the baking dish from the oven and let the custards cool in the water bath for 5 minutes. Transfer the ramekins to a wire rack to cool completely. Refrigerate for at least 4 hours to chill. Serve chilled, topped with whipped cream (if using). Cover any leftovers with plastic wrap and refrigerate for up to 3 days.

ESPRESSO PANNA COTTA

Serves 4

PREP TIME: 15 minutes
COOK TIME: 5 minutes
CHILLING TIME: 4 hours
EQIPMENT: Small saucepan, 4 (6-ounce) ramekins

Ingredients:

- 1 cup whole milk
- 1 tablespoon unflavored powdered gelatin
- 3 cups heavy (whipping) cream
- ½ cup sugar
- 2 tablespoons instant espresso powder
- Pinch salt
- Dark chocolate shavings, for garnish (optional)

Directions:

4. In a small saucepan, add the milk and sprinkle the gelatin over it. Let sit for 5 minutes. Place the pan over medium heat and gently heat for about 2 minutes, stirring frequently, until the gelatin dissolves.

5. Stir in the cream, sugar, espresso powder, and salt. Turn the heat to low and continue to heat for about 3 minutes more, just until the sugar dissolves. Spoon the mixture into 4 (6-ounce) ramekins or custard cups, dividing equally. Cover and refrigerate, stirring once or twice during the first hour of chilling. Let chill for at least 4 hours.

6. Serve chilled, garnished with chocolate shavings (if using). Refrigerate any leftovers (see tip).

STRAWBERRY CLAFOUTIS

Serves 6

PREP TIME: 15 minutes
COOK TIME: 30 minutes
EQIPMENT: 9-inch round baking dish or pie dish, whisk

Ingredients:

- 3 tablespoons unsalted butter, melted, plus more for preparing the pan
- ½ cup all-purpose flour
- ¼ cup plus 2 tablespoons sugar
- Pinch salt
- 3 eggs
- Finely grated zest of 1 lemon
- ¼ cup plus 2 tablespoons low-fat or whole milk
- 3 cups halved or quartered fresh strawberries (about 1½ pints)
- Powdered sugar, for garnish

Directions:

8. Preheat the oven to 350°F.

9. Generously grease a 9-inch round baking dish or pie dish with butter.

10. In a large bowl, whisk the flour, sugar, and salt.

11. Add the eggs, melted butter, and lemon zest. Whisk until smooth.

12. Add the milk and continue whisking for about 3 minutes more until the mixture is smooth and light.

13. Arrange the strawberries in an even layer in the bottom of the prepared dish and pour the batter over the top. Bake for about 30 minutes until the top is golden and the center is set.

14. Remove from the oven and let cool for a few minutes. Dust with powdered sugar, slice into wedges, and serve immediately. Cover any leftovers with plastic wrap and refrigerate for up to 3 days.

KEY LIME MOUSSE PIE CUPS

Serves 10

PREP TIME: 15 minutes

CHILLING TIME: 1 hour

EQIPMENT: 10 (4-ounce) ramekins or custard cups, electric mixer

Ingredients:

- ⅔ cup graham cracker crumbs
- 2 teaspoons sugar
- 2 tablespoons unsalted butter, melted
- 2 cups cold heavy (whipping) cream
- 1 (14-ounce) can sweetened condensed milk
- ½ cup freshly squeezed key lime juice (from about 14 key limes)
- Lime zest (optional)

Directions:

4. In a small bowl, combine the graham cracker crumbs, sugar, and melted butter. Stir to mix well. Divide the mixture equally among 10 (4-ounce) ramekins or custard cups.

5. In a large bowl, using an electric mixer, whip the cream until stiff peaks form.

6. In another small bowl, whisk the sweetened condensed milk and lime juice. Gently fold the lime juice mixture into the whipped cream until incorporated. Spoon the mixture into the ramekins or custard cups on top of the graham cracker crust. Chill thoroughly, for at least 1 hour, and serve cold, garnished with the lime zest, if desired. Cover any leftovers with plastic wrap and refrigerate for up to 3 days.

Serves 12

PREP TIME: 20 minutes

COOK TIME: 32 to 35 minutes

COOLING AND **CHILLING TIME:** 3 hours, 30 minutes

EQIPMENT: 9-by-13-inch baking pan, electric mixer

Ingredients:

- Unsalted butter, for preparing the baking pan
- All-purpose flour, for preparing the baking pan

FOR THE CAKE

- 5 eggs, separated
- 1 cup sugar, divided
- ⅓ cup whole milk
- 1 teaspoon vanilla extract
- 1 cup all-purpose flour
- 1½ teaspoons baking powder
- ¼ teaspoon salt

FOR THE FILLING

- 1 (14-ounce) can sweetened condensed milk
- 1 (12-ounce) can evaporated milk
- ½ cup heavy (whipping) cream

FOR THE WHIPPED CREAM TOPPING

- 1 pint heavy (whipping) cream
- 3 tablespoons powdered sugar
- Ground cinnamon, for garnish

Directions:

TO MAKE THE CAKE

1. Preheat the oven to 350°F.
2. Line a 9-by-13-inch pan with aluminum foil, and grease and flour the foil.
3. In a large bowl, using a handheld electric mixer or in a stand mixer on medium-high speed, beat together the egg yolks and ½ cup of sugar for about 4 minutes until the mixture becomes pale and doubles in volume.
4. Add the milk, vanilla, flour, baking powder, and salt. Turn the speed to low and beat until just combined.
5. In a medium bowl using a handheld electric mixer or a stand mixer on high speed, whip the egg whites until they hold soft peaks. Slowly add the remaining ½ cup of sugar and continue to whip on high speed until the mixture holds stiff peaks. Using a rubber spatula, gently fold the whipped egg whites into the cake batter. Transfer the batter to the prepared pan and bake for 32 to 35 minutes until springy to the touch and a toothpick inserted in the center comes out clean.
6. Remove from the oven and set the pan on a wire rack to cool for 30 minutes.

TO MAKE THE FILLING

1. In a medium bowl, stir together the sweetened condensed milk, evaporated milk, and cream until well combined.
2. Using a fork, poke holes all over the cake. Pour the filling over the top of the cake letting it seep into the holes.
3. Let the cake cool for at least 1 hour. Cover and refrigerate for at least 2 hours or overnight.

TO MAKE THE WHIPPED CREAM TOPPING

1. In a large bowl, using a handheld electric mixer or in a stand mixer on high speed, whip the heavy cream until soft peaks form.
2. Add the powdered sugar and beat until the mixture is well combined and reaches a thick, spreadable consistency. Spoon the whipped cream topping over the cake, smoothing it with a spatula.
3. Dust with cinnamon and serve immediately.

BOURBON-CHOCOLATE BUNDT CAKE

Serves 12

PREP TIME: 15 minutes
COOK TIME: 40 to 50 minutes
COOLING TIME: 2 hours
EQIPMENT: 10-inch Bundt pan
Ingredients:

- 1 cup plus 3 tablespoons unsweetened cocoa powder, divided
- 1½ cups brewed coffee
- ½ cup bourbon whiskey
- 1 cup (2 sticks) unsalted butter, cut into 1-inch pieces, plus more for preparing the pan
- 2 cups sugar
- 2 cups all-purpose flour
- 1¼ teaspoons baking soda
- ½ teaspoon salt
- 2 eggs
- 1 teaspoon vanilla extract
- Powdered sugar, for garnish

Directions:

1. Preheat the oven to 325°F.
2. Grease a 10-inch Bundt pan and dust it with 3 tablespoons of cocoa powder.
3. In a medium saucepan set over medium heat, whisk the coffee, bourbon, butter, and remaining 1 cup of cocoa powder until the butter melts. Remove the pan from the heat and whisk in the sugar until it dissolves. Pour the mixture into a large bowl and let cool for several minutes.
4. Meanwhile, in another large bowl, whisk the flour, baking soda, and salt.
5. In a small bowl, whisk the eggs and vanilla. Add the egg mixture to the chocolate mixture once it has cooled a bit and whisk well to combine.
6. Add the flour mixture and whisk to combine. Transfer the batter to the prepared pan and bake for 40 to 50 minutes until a toothpick inserted into the center comes out clean.
7. Remove the cake from the oven and set it, in the pan, on a wire rack to cool completely. Use a sharp knife to loosen the edges of the cake from the pan sides and then invert the cake onto a serving platter.
8. Dust with powdered sugar and serve.

MOLTEN CHOCOLATE LAVA CAKES

Serves 4

PREP TIME: 10 minutes
COOK TIME: 12 to 14 minutes
EQIPMENT: 4 (6-ounce) ramekins or custard cups
Ingredients:

- Nonstick baking spray

- ½ cup (1 stick) unsalted butter
- 4 ounces semisweet chocolate, chopped
- 1¼ cups powdered sugar, plus more for garnish
- 3 egg yolks
- 2 eggs
- 1 teaspoon vanilla extract
- ½ cup all-purpose flour

Directions:

1. Preheat the oven to 425°F.
2. Spray 4 (6-ounce) ramekins or custard cups with nonstick baking spray and place them on a baking sheet.
3. In a large microwave-safe bowl, combine the butter and chocolate. Microwave at 50 percent power for about 1 minute until the butter melts. Whisk until the chocolate is completely melted and the mixture is smooth.
4. Add the powdered sugar and stir to combine.
5. In a small bowl, whisk the egg yolks and eggs and add them to the chocolate mixture along with the vanilla. Stir the batter to combine thoroughly.
6. Add the flour and stir to mix. Scoop the batter into the prepared ramekins, dividing equally. Transfer the baking sheet with the filled ramekins to the oven and bake for 12 to 14 minutes until the edges are firm, but the centers are still soft.
7. Remove from the oven and let cool for 1 minute. Run a sharp knife around the inside of each ramekin and then invert each onto a serving plate.
8. Dust the tops with powdered sugar and serve immediately.

LEMON CHEESECAKE

Serves 10

PREP TIME: 15 minutes

CHILLING TIME: 5 hours

EQIPMENT: Electric mixer, 9-inch springform pan

Ingredients:

- 1½ cups finely ground graham cracker crumbs (from about 9 graham crackers)
- ¼ cup packed brown sugar
- 6 tablespoons (¾ stick) unsalted butter, melted
- 1 cup heavy (whipping) cream
- 8 ounces cream cheese, at room temperature
- ½ cup lemon curd
- ⅓ cup powdered sugar
- 1 teaspoon vanilla extract

Directions:

1. In a medium bowl, stir together the graham cracker crumbs, brown sugar, and butter until well combined. Press the mixture into the bottom and a bit up the sides of a 9-inch springform pan in an even

layer. Refrigerate for 1 hour.

2. In a large bowl, using a handheld electric mixer or in a stand mixer, whip the cream until it holds stiff peaks.

3. In another large bowl, beat the cream cheese until it is creamy and smooth.

4. Beat the lemon curd, powdered sugar, and vanilla into the cream cheese.

5. Using a rubber spatula, gently fold in the whipped cream. Spoon the mixture into the prepared crust and use the rubber spatula to smooth the top. Refrigerate for at least 4 hours until completely set. Serve chilled.

S'MORES CUPS

Makes 12 cups

PREP TIME: 15 minutes

COOK TIME: 10 minutes

EQIPMENT: 12-cup muffin tin, foil cupcake liners

Ingredients:

- Nonstick baking spray
- 10 graham crackers, crushed (about 2 cups)
- ½ cup (1 stick) plus 1 tablespoon unsalted butter, melted
- ½ cup sugar
- ¾ cup semisweet chocolate chips
- 1½ cups mini marshmallows

Directions:

1. Preheat the oven to 350°F.

2. Line a 12-cup muffin tin with foil liners. Spray the inside of the liners with nonstick baking spray. You can skip the liners if you like and just spray the tin, but the s'mores may crumble a bit when removed from the pan.

3. In a medium bowl, stir together the graham cracker crumbs, butter, and sugar until thoroughly combined. Put about 2 tablespoons of the mixture into each muffin cup and press it firmly into the bottom of the cup. Bake for 5 minutes.

4. Remove the muffin tin from the oven and let cool. Leave the oven on.

5. Divide half the chocolate chips and half the marshmallows evenly among the cups. Top the marshmallows with a second layer of graham cracker crumbs, about 1½ to 2 tablespoons of crumbs in each cup. Press down firmly to pack the crumb mixture. Return to the oven and bake for 4 minutes.

6. Remove the muffin tin from the oven and turn on the broiler. Add the remaining chocolate chips and marshmallows to the cups, dividing equally, and put the pan under the broiler for 2 to 3 minutes until the marshmallows are toasted and golden brown.

7. Remove from the oven and let the cups cool in the pan for 15 minutes before removing them from the tin to a wire rack to cool completely.

PEANUT BRITTLE

Serves 10

PREP TIME: 20 minutes

COOLING TIME: 1 to 2 hours
EQIPMENT: Baking sheet
Ingredients:

- Nonstick baking spray
- 1 cup sugar
- ½ cup light corn syrup
- 1 cup unsalted peanuts
- ¼ teaspoon salt
- 1 tablespoon unsalted butter
- 1 teaspoon vanilla extract
- 1 teaspoon baking soda

Directions:

7. Spray a baking sheet with nonstick baking spray.
8. In a large microwave-safe bowl, whisk the sugar and corn syrup. Microwave at full power for 4 minutes.
9. Stir in the peanuts and salt to combine. Microwave again at full power for 3½ minutes.
10. Stir in the butter and vanilla until the butter melts completely. Return to the microwave and microwave at full power for 1½ minutes more.
11. Immediately stir in the baking soda. The mixture will foam up. Transfer the mixture to the prepared sheet, and with a rubber spatula, gently spread it into an even layer.
12. Let cool completely for 1 to 2 hours. To serve, break the brittle into pieces.

WITH FLAKY SEA SALT

Makes 12 cupcakes

PREP TIME: 10 minutes
BAKE TIME: 18 to 20 minutes
EQIPMENT: 12-cup muffin tin, paper cupcake liners
Ingredients:
FOR THE CUPCAKES

- 1½ cups all-purpose flour
- 1½ teaspoons baking powder
- ¼ teaspoon salt
- ½ cup (1 stick) unsalted butter, at room temperature
- ¼ cup granulated sugar
- ½ cup packed dark brown sugar
- 1 teaspoon vanilla extract
- 2 eggs
- ½ cup low-fat or whole milk

FOR THE FROSTING

- ½ cup (1 stick) unsalted butter, at room temperature

- 1 cup packed dark brown sugar
- ⅓ cup heavy (whipping) cream
- ½ teaspoon salt
- 2 to 2½ cups powdered sugar
- 1 teaspoon flaky sea salt

Directions:

TO MAKE THE CUPCAKES

8. Preheat the oven to 350°F.
9. Line a 12-cup muffin tin with paper liners.
10. In a medium bowl, combine the flour, baking powder, and salt.
11. In a large bowl, with a handheld electric mixer or stand mixer, cream together the butter, granulated sugar, and brown sugar for about 3 minutes until pale and fluffy.
12. Add the vanilla and eggs and beat to combine.
13. Add the dry ingredients and the milk in alternating batches, beating to combine after each addition. Scoop the batter into the prepared muffin tin. Bake for 18 to 20 minutes until a toothpick inserted into the center of one of the cupcakes comes out clean.
14. Remove from the oven and let the cupcakes cool in the pan for a few minutes before removing them from the tin to a wire rack to cool completely.

TO MAKE THE FROSTING

5. While the cupcakes cool, make the frosting. In a small saucepan over medium heat, melt the butter. Add the brown sugar, cream, and salt. Cook for about 4 minutes, stirring, until the sugar dissolves completely. Remove from the heat and let cool.
6. In a large bowl, using a handheld electric mixer or in a stand mixer, combine the brown sugar mixture with 2 cups of powdered sugar and beat on medium speed for 5 minutes until thick. Add more powdered sugar as needed to get a thick, spreadable consistency.
7. When the cupcakes are cool, pipe, spread, or scoop the frosting onto them.
8. Sprinkle with flaky sea salt to garnish. Serve at room temperature.

WITH WHITE CHOCOLATE–ORANGE BUTTERCREAM

Makes 12 cupcakes

PREP TIME: 30 minutes

COOK TIME: 18 to 20 minutes

EQIPMENT: 12-cup muffin tin, paper cupcake liners (preferably dark pink in color)

Ingredients:

FOR THE CUPCAKES

- 1 cup all-purpose flour
- ¾ cup unsweetened Dutch process cocoa powder
- 1 teaspoon baking powder
- ¼ teaspoon salt
- ½ cup (1 stick) unsalted butter, at room temperature

- 1 cup plus 3 tablespoons sugar, divided
- 2 teaspoons vanilla extract
- 2 eggs
- ½ cup sour cream
- Juice of 1 orange (see tip)

FOR THE BUTTERCREAM

- 2 ounces white chocolate
- 5 tablespoons unsalted butter, at room temperature
- 2 cups powdered sugar
- Zest of 1 orange

Directions:

TO MAKE THE CUPCAKES

9. Preheat the oven to 350°F.
10. Line a 12-cup muffin tin with dark pink paper liners.
11. In a medium bowl, stir together the flour, cocoa powder, baking powder, and salt.
12. In a large bowl, using an electric mixer or in a stand mixer, beat together the butter and 1 cup of sugar on high speed until light and fluffy.
13. Add the vanilla, eggs, and sour cream and beat until incorporated.
14. Add the flour mixture in 2 batches, beating after each addition until incorporated. Scoop the batter into the prepared muffin tin and bake for 18 to 20 minutes until a toothpick inserted into the center of one of the cupcakes comes out clean.
15. Remove from the oven and let the cupcakes cool for a couple of minutes before removing them from the tin to a wire rack to cool completely.
16. Meanwhile, in a small bowl, stir together the orange juice and remaining 3 tablespoons of sugar. Drizzle the mixture over the warm cupcakes and let them cool completely.

TO MAKE THE BUTTERCREAM

6. In a small microwave-safe bowl, microwave the white chocolate at 50 percent power, in 30-second intervals, stirring in between, until completely melted and smooth.
7. In a medium bowl, beat the butter until light and fluffy.
8. Add the powdered sugar to the butter in 2 or 3 batches, beating after each addition until well combined. Continue to beat for about 5 minutes until thick and smooth.
9. Add the melted chocolate and orange zest and beat to incorporate.
10. Pipe, spread, or scoop the frosting onto the cooled cupcakes.

RED VELVET CUPCAKES

Makes 12 cupcakes

PREP TIME: 20 minutes
COOK TIME: 18 to 20 minutes
EQIPMENT: 12-cup muffin tin, paper cupcake liners
Ingredients:
FOR THE CUPCAKES

- 4 tablespoons (½ stick) unsalted butter, at room temperature
- ¾ cup sugar
- 1 egg
- 2½ tablespoons unsweetened cocoa powder
- 3 tablespoons red food coloring
- ½ teaspoon vanilla extract
- ½ cup buttermilk
- 1 cup plus 2 tablespoons all-purpose flour
- 1½ teaspoons distilled white vinegar
- ½ teaspoon salt
- ½ teaspoon baking soda

FOR THE FROSTING

- ½ cup (1 stick) unsalted butter, at room temperature
- 4 ounces cream cheese, at room temperature
- 2½ cups powdered sugar
- 1 tablespoon vanilla extract

Directions:

TO MAKE THE CUPCAKES

9. Preheat the oven to 350°F.
10. Line a 12-cup muffin tin with paper liners.
11. In a large bowl, with a handheld electric mixer or in a stand mixer, cream together the butter and sugar on medium speed for about 3 minutes until the mixture becomes pale and fluffy.
12. Add the egg and beat on high speed to incorporate.
13. In a small bowl, stir together the cocoa powder, food coloring, and vanilla. Add this mixture to the batter and beat on medium speed to combine well.
14. With the mixer running on low speed, add the buttermilk and flour in alternating batches, beating to combine after each addition. Turn the mixer to high speed and beat until smooth.
15. Add the vinegar, salt, and baking soda. Beat for 2 minutes more. Scoop the batter into the prepared muffin tin. Bake for 18 to 20 minutes until a toothpick inserted into the center of one of the cupcakes comes out clean.
16. Remove from the oven and let the cupcakes cool in the pan for several minutes before removing them from the tin to a wire rack to cool completely.

TO MAKE THE FROSTING

5. In a large bowl, with a handheld electric mixer or in a stand mixer fitted with a whisk attachment, whip the butter and cream cheese for about 5 minutes until smooth.
6. With the mixer running on low speed, slowly add the powdered sugar, beating until thoroughly incorporated.
7. Add the vanilla and whip the frosting on medium-high speed until fluffy and light.
8. When the cupcakes are cool, pipe, spread, or scoop the frosting onto them and serve at room temperature.

TRES LECHES CAKE

Serves 12

PREP TIME: 20 minutes

COOK TIME: 32 to 35 minutes

COOLING AND **CHILLING TIME:** 3 hours, 30 minutes

EQIPMENT: 9-by-13-inch baking pan, electric mixer

Ingredients:

- Unsalted butter, for preparing the baking pan
- All-purpose flour, for preparing the baking pan

FOR THE CAKE

- 5 eggs, separated
- 1 cup sugar, divided
- ⅓ cup whole milk
- 1 teaspoon vanilla extract
- 1 cup all-purpose flour
- 1½ teaspoons baking powder
- ¼ teaspoon salt

FOR THE FILLING

- 1 (14-ounce) can sweetened condensed milk
- 1 (12-ounce) can evaporated milk
- ½ cup heavy (whipping) cream

FOR THE WHIPPED CREAM TOPPING

- 1 pint heavy (whipping) cream
- 3 tablespoons powdered sugar
- Ground cinnamon, for garnish

Directions:

TO MAKE THE CAKE

7. Preheat the oven to 350°F.
8. Line a 9-by-13-inch pan with aluminum foil, and grease and flour the foil.
9. In a large bowl, using a handheld electric mixer or in a stand mixer on medium-high speed, beat together the egg yolks and ½ cup of sugar for about 4 minutes until the mixture becomes pale and doubles in volume.
10. Add the milk, vanilla, flour, baking powder, and salt. Turn the speed to low and beat until just combined.
11. In a medium bowl using a handheld electric mixer or a stand mixer on high speed, whip the egg whites until they hold soft peaks. Slowly add the remaining ½ cup of sugar and continue to whip on high speed until the mixture holds stiff peaks. Using a rubber spatula, gently fold the whipped egg whites into the cake batter. Transfer the batter to the prepared pan and bake for 32 to 35 minutes until springy to the touch and a toothpick inserted in the center comes out clean.
12. Remove from the oven and set the pan on a wire rack to cool for 30 minutes.

TO MAKE THE FILLING

4. In a medium bowl, stir together the sweetened condensed milk, evaporated milk, and cream until well combined.

5. Using a fork, poke holes all over the cake. Pour the filling over the top of the cake letting it seep into the holes.

6. Let the cake cool for at least 1 hour. Cover and refrigerate for at least 2 hours or overnight.

TO MAKE THE WHIPPED CREAM TOPPING

4. In a large bowl, using a handheld electric mixer or in a stand mixer on high speed, whip the heavy cream until soft peaks form.

5. Add the powdered sugar and beat until the mixture is well combined and reaches a thick, spreadable consistency. Spoon the whipped cream topping over the cake, smoothing it with a spatula.

6. Dust with cinnamon and serve immediately.

BOURBON-CHOCOLATE BUNDT CAKE

Serves 12

PREP TIME: 15 minutes
COOK TIME: 40 to 50 minutes
COOLING TIME: 2 hours
EQIPMENT: 10-inch Bundt pan

Ingredients:

- 1 cup plus 3 tablespoons unsweetened cocoa powder, divided
- 1½ cups brewed coffee
- ½ cup bourbon whiskey
- 1 cup (2 sticks) unsalted butter, cut into 1-inch pieces, plus more for preparing the pan
- 2 cups sugar
- 2 cups all-purpose flour
- 1¼ teaspoons baking soda
- ½ teaspoon salt
- 2 eggs
- 1 teaspoon vanilla extract
- Powdered sugar, for garnish

Directions:

9. Preheat the oven to 325°F.

10. Grease a 10-inch Bundt pan and dust it with 3 tablespoons of cocoa powder.

11. In a medium saucepan set over medium heat, whisk the coffee, bourbon, butter, and remaining 1 cup of cocoa powder until the butter melts. Remove the pan from the heat and whisk in the sugar until it dissolves. Pour the mixture into a large bowl and let cool for several minutes.

12. Meanwhile, in another large bowl, whisk the flour, baking soda, and salt.

13. In a small bowl, whisk the eggs and vanilla. Add the egg mixture to the chocolate mixture once it has cooled a bit and whisk well to combine.

14. Add the flour mixture and whisk to combine. Transfer the batter to the prepared pan and bake for 40 to

50 minutes until a toothpick inserted into the center comes out clean.

15. Remove the cake from the oven and set it, in the pan, on a wire rack to cool completely. Use a sharp knife to loosen the edges of the cake from the pan sides and then invert the cake onto a serving platter.

16. Dust with powdered sugar and serve.

CHOCOLATE MOUSSE

Serves 8

PREP TIME: 15 minutes
CHILLING TIME: 4 hours
EQIPMENT: Small saucepan, electric mixer with whisk attachment
Ingredients:

- 2 eggs
- ¼ cup sugar
- 2½ cups cold heavy (whipping) cream, divided
- 6 ounces semisweet chocolate, chopped

Directions:

7. In a large bowl, using an electric mixer, beat together the eggs and sugar for 3 minutes.
8. In a small saucepan set over medium heat, bring 1 cup of cream to a simmer. Do not let it boil.
9. With the mixer running, add the hot cream to the egg mixture in a slow, steady stream until it is thoroughly incorporated. Transfer the egg and cream mixture to the saucepan and place it over low heat. Cook for about 5 minutes, stirring constantly, until the mixture thickens.
10. Remove the pan from the heat and add the chocolate. Stir until the chocolate is completely melted and incorporated. Refrigerate, covered, for at least 2 hours, stirring occasionally.
11. When the mixture is fully chilled, use an electric mixer with a whisk attachment to whip the remaining 1½ cups of cream until stiff peaks form. Add the whipped cream to the chilled chocolate mixture, gently folding, until it is fully incorporated and the mixture is smooth.
12. Cover with plastic wrap and refrigerate for at least 2 hours to chill. Serve chilled. Cover any leftovers with plastic wrap and refrigerate for up to 3 days.

PEACHES AND CREAM

Serves 4

PREP TIME: 10 minutes
CHILLING TIME: 2 hours
EQIPMENT: Blender or food processor, 4 (8-ounce) ramekins, custard cups, or wineglasses
Ingredients:

- 3 tablespoons cold water
- 2¼ teaspoons (1 envelope) unflavored gelatin
- 5 cups diced peaches, divided
- ½ cup plus 2 teaspoons sugar, divided
- 1 teaspoon vanilla extract
- ¾ cup sour cream

Directions:

6. In a small microwave-safe bowl, stir together the water and gelatin. Microwave on high power for 20 seconds and stir. If the gelatin is not fully dissolved, return to the microwave for another 10 seconds on high power.

7. In a blender or food processor, combine 4 cups of peaches with ½ cup of the sugar and the vanilla. Process until smooth.

8. Add the sour cream and pulse to incorporate.

9. With the motor running on low, add the gelatin mixture in a slow steady stream. Divide the mixture evenly between 4 (8-ounce) ramekins, custard cups, or wineglasses, cover, and refrigerate for at least 2 hours, until set.

10. Before serving, in a small bowl, toss together the remaining 1 cup of diced peaches with the remaining 2 teaspoons of sugar and let macerate for about 2 minutes. Top each serving with some of the diced peaches and serve immediately. Cover any leftovers with plastic wrap and refrigerate for up to 3 days.

WHITE CHOCOLATE–RASPBERRY SWIRL CHEESECAKE

Serves 10

PREP TIME: 20 minutes
COOK TIME: 35 to 40 minutes
CHILLING TIME: 3 hours
EQIPMENT: Electric mixer, 9-inch springform pan

Ingredients:

- 2 cups chocolate wafer cookie crumbs (I prefer Nabisco Famous Chocolate Wafers)
- 4 tablespoons (½ stick) unsalted butter, melted
- 2 (8-ounce) packages cream cheese, at room temperature
- ½ cup sugar
- ½ teaspoon vanilla extract
- 2 eggs
- 3 ounces white chocolate, melted
- 3 tablespoons raspberry preserves

Directions:

8. Preheat the oven to 350°F.

9. In a small bowl, combine the cookie crumbs and melted butter. Press the mixture into the bottom and partway up the sides of a 9-inch springform pan.

10. In a medium bowl, using a handheld electric mixer or in a stand mixer, beat together the cream cheese, sugar, and vanilla.

11. Add the eggs and beat until just combined.

12. Stir in the white chocolate and pour the batter into the prepared crust.

13. Put the preserves in a small microwave-safe bowl and microwave at high power for about 20 seconds to melt. Using a small spoon, dollop the preserves on top of the cheesecake. Use the tip of a knife to drag and swirl the preserves through the batter. Bake for 35 to 40 minutes until the center is mostly set.

14. Remove from the oven and let cool. Refrigerate for at least 3 hours before serving.

BLACKBERRY CRUMB CAKE

Serves 8

PREP TIME: 10 minutes

COOK TIME: 45 minutes

EQIPMENT: Electric mixer, 8-inch square or round cake pan

Ingredients:

FOR THE TOPPING

- ½ cup old-fashioned rolled oats
- ½ cup packed brown sugar
- ¼ cup all-purpose flour
- 4 tablespoons (½ stick) cold unsalted butter

FOR THE CAKE

- 4 tablespoons (½ stick) unsalted butter, at room temperature, plus more for preparing the baking pan
- 1¾ cups all-purpose flour, plus more for preparing the baking pan
- ¾ cup sugar
- 1 egg
- 1 teaspoon vanilla extract
- Zest of 1 lemon
- 2 teaspoons baking powder
- ½ teaspoon salt
- ½ cup low-fat or whole milk
- 2 heaping cups fresh blackberries, halved if large

Directions:

TO MAKE THE TOPPING

2. In a medium bowl, stir together the oats, brown sugar, and flour. Using your fingers, mix in the butter until it is incorporated and the mixture forms coarse crumbs.

TO MAKE THE CAKE

9. Preheat the oven to 375°F.

10. Butter and flour an 8-inch cake pan. Line the pan with parchment paper, using enough that it hangs over the sides (to make cake removal easier).

11. In a large bowl, using a handheld electric mixer or a stand mixer, cream together the butter and sugar until fluffy and light.

12. Add the egg, vanilla, and lemon zest and mix to incorporate.

13. In a medium bowl, combine the flour, baking powder, and salt.

14. Add the dry ingredients and the milk to the wet ingredients in 3 alternating batches (one-third of the dry mixture followed by one-third of the milk), stirring in between to incorporate.

15. Fold in the blackberries. Transfer the batter to the prepared pan and sprinkle the topping evenly over the batter. Bake for about 45 minutes until a toothpick inserted into the center comes out clean.

16. Remove from the oven and let the cake cool in the pan. Lift the cake out of the pan, cut it into squares or

wedges, and serve.

PEACH UPSIDE-DOWN CAKE

Serves 8

PREP TIME: 15 minutes
COOK TIME: 45 to 50 minutes
EQIPMENT: 9-inch round cake pan
Ingredients:

- Unsalted butter, for preparing the pan

FOR THE TOPPING

- ½ cup packed brown sugar
- 4 tablespoons (½ stick) unsalted butter, melted
- 5 peaches, peeled and cut into ¼-inch thick slices

FOR THE CAKE

- 1 ⅓ cups all-purpose flour
- 1½ teaspoons baking powder
- ¼ teaspoon salt
- ½ cup (1 stick) unsalted butter, at room temperature
- ⅓ cup granulated sugar
- ⅓ cup packed brown sugar
- 1 egg
- ¼ cup low-fat or whole milk
- 2 teaspoons vanilla extract

Directions:

2. Grease the bottom and sides of a 9-inch round cake pan with butter.

TO MAKE THE TOPPING

3. In a small bowl, mix together the brown sugar and melted butter. Spread it into the bottom of the prepared pan.
4. Starting from the middle of the pan, arrange the peach slices, covering the entire surface and layering the fruit as needed.

TO MAKE THE CAKE

7. Preheat the oven to 350°F.
8. In a small bowl, stir together the flour, baking powder, and salt.
9. In a medium bowl, with a handheld electric mixer, a stand mixer, or a wooden spoon, cream together the butter, granulated sugar, and brown sugar.
10. Add the egg, milk, and vanilla. Beat to mix well.
11. Add the dry ingredients and beat on low speed until fully incorporated. Spoon the batter evenly over the peaches and carefully smooth it into an even layer. Bake for 45 to 50 minutes until golden brown and springy to the touch.
12. Remove from the oven and let the cake cool in the pan for 5 minutes. To unmold the cake, run a sharp knife around the edge of the pan and place an inverted serving platter on top. Carefully invert the cake

so it falls out onto the platter. Slice into wedges and serve.

PINEAPPLE UPSIDE-DOWN CUPCAKES

Makes 12 cupcakes

PREP TIME: 15 minutes

COOK TIME: 24 to 26 minutes

EQIPMENT: 12-cup muffin tin, electric mixer

Ingredients:

- Nonstick baking spray
- 1 (20-ounce) can and 1 (8-ounce) can pineapple chunks in juice, drained with ½ cup juice reserved
- ⅓ cup packed brown sugar
- ⅓ cup unsalted butter, melted, plus 4 tablespoons (½ stick), at room temperature
- 1 cup all-purpose flour
- ¾ cup plus 2 tablespoons granulated sugar, divided
- ½ teaspoon baking powder
- ¼ teaspoon salt
- 1 egg
- ½ teaspoon vanilla extract
- ¾ cup heavy (whipping) cream
- 12 maraschino cherries

Directions:

11. Preheat the oven to 350°F.
12. Spray a 12-cup muffin tin with nonstick baking spray.
13. Place several layers of paper towels on a plate and spread the drained pineapple chunks on top to drain thoroughly.
14. In a small bowl, stir together the brown sugar and melted butter. Spoon the mixture into the muffin cups, coating the bottom of each with about 2 teaspoons of the mixture.
15. Arrange about 5 pineapple chunks in a single layer in the bottom of each muffin cup.
16. In a large bowl, using a handheld electric mixer or a stand mixer, combine the flour, ¾ cup of granulated sugar, the baking powder, and salt.
17. Add the room temperature butter and the reserved ½ cup of pineapple juice and beat for 1 to 2 minutes.
18. Add the egg and vanilla and beat until just incorporated. Scoop the batter into the muffin cups over the pineapple chunks, filling each cup ¾ of the way full. Bake for 24 to 26 minutes, or until a toothpick inserted into the center of one of the cupcakes comes out clean.
19. Remove from the oven and let the cupcakes cool in the tin for about 5 minutes. To remove the cupcakes, run a sharp knife around the edge of each cup to loosen the cupcakes, and place a wire rack on top of the muffin tin and carefully invert it. The cupcakes should fall out onto the rack. Let the cupcakes cool completely on the rack before topping them.
20. While the cupcakes cool, in a large bowl, using an electric mixer with a whisk attachment or by hand using a whisk, whip the cream and remaining 2 tablespoons of granulated sugar until the cream holds stiff peaks. Dollop or pipe the whipped cream onto the cupcakes and top each with a maraschino cherry.

WITH COCONUT BUTTERCREAM FROSTING

Makes 12 cupcakes

PREP TIME: 20 minutes

COOK TIME: 18 to 20 minutes

EQIPMENT: 12-cup muffin tin, paper cupcake liners, electric mixer

Ingredients:

FOR THE CUPCAKES

- 1 cup all-purpose flour
- 1¼ teaspoons baking powder
- ¼ teaspoon salt
- ½ cup (1 stick) unsalted butter, at room temperature
- ¾ cup sugar
- 1 egg, at room temperature
- 1 egg white, at room temperature
- 1 teaspoon vanilla extract
- 1 teaspoon coconut extract
- ½ cup full-fat canned coconut milk

FOR THE FROSTING

- ¾ cup unsalted butter, kept at room temperature for 25 to 30 minutes before using
- 6 tablespoons full-fat canned coconut milk
- 2½ to 3 cups powdered sugar
- 1 teaspoon coconut extract
- 1 cup sweetened shredded coconut

Directions:

TO MAKE THE CUPCAKES

8. Preheat the oven to 350°F.

9. Line a 12-cup muffin tin with paper liners.

10. In a medium bowl, combine the flour, baking powder, and salt.

11. In a large bowl, using a handheld electric mixer or a stand mixer set on medium speed, cream together the butter and sugar for about 3 minutes until fluffy and pale.

12. Add the egg, egg white, and vanilla. Mix well to combine.

13. With the mixer on low speed, add the dry ingredients, coconut extract, and coconut milk in alternating batches, beating well after each addition. Scoop the batter into the prepared muffin tin, dividing equally. Bake for 18 to 20 minutes until a toothpick inserted into the center of one of the cupcakes comes out clean.

14. Remove from the oven and let the cupcakes cool in the pan for 10 minutes before removing them from the tin to a wire rack to cool completely.

TO MAKE THE FROSTING

5. In a large bowl, using a handheld electric mixer or a stand mixer, beat together the butter and coconut milk until creamy.

6. Add 2½ cups of powdered sugar and beat on medium-low speed until combined. Raise the speed to medium-high and continue to beat until the mixture is fluffy and light.

7. Add the coconut extract and more powdered sugar as needed to get a thick, spreadable consistency.

8. Once the cupcakes are completely cool, pipe or spread the frosting on top and sprinkle with the shredded coconut. Serve at room temperature.

ORANGE SHERBET

Serves 8

PREP TIME: 10 minutes

CHILLING AND FREEZING TIME: 5 hours

EQIPMENT: Freezer-safe storage container

Ingredients:

- ½ cup sugar
- ½ cup frozen orange juice concentrate, thawed or partially thawed
- 2 cups freshly squeezed orange juice
- 1½ cups whole milk
- 2 tablespoons freshly squeezed lemon juice
- 1 tablespoon vanilla extract
- ¼ teaspoon salt

Directions:

4. In a medium bowl, stir together the sugar, orange juice concentrate, orange juice, milk, lemon juice, vanilla, and salt until well combined and smooth. Refrigerate the mixture for at least 2 hours until fully chilled.

5. Pour the mixture into a freezer-safe storage container, cover with plastic wrap, and freeze for about 45 minutes before checking on it the first time. As soon as it begins to freeze around the edges, mix it vigorously with a whisk, spatula, wooden spoon, or ideally, a handheld electric mixer or immersion blender. Continue to freeze, mixing it every 30 minutes until it is fully frozen, about 3 hours total.

6. Store in the freezer until ready to serve.

CHOCOLATE CHIP COOKIES

Makes about 24 cookies

PREP TIME: 10 minutes

BAKE TIME: 9 to 11 minutes

EQIPMENT: Baking sheet

Ingredients:

- ½ cup (1 stick) unsalted butter, melted
- ½ cup granulated sugar
- ¼ cup packed light brown sugar
- 1 teaspoon vanilla extract
- 1 egg

- 1½ cups all-purpose flour
- ¾ teaspoon salt
- ½ teaspoon baking soda
- ¾ cup semisweet chocolate chips

Directions

7. Preheat the oven to 350°F.
8. In a large bowl, with a wooden spoon, electric mixer, or in the bowl of a stand mixer, cream together the butter, granulated sugar, and brown sugar until creamy.
9. Add the vanilla and egg. Mix just until incorporated.
10. Add the flour, salt, and baking soda. Mix until the mixture clumps.
11. Mix in the chocolate chips. Drop the batter by rounded tablespoons onto an ungreased baking sheet, leaving about 2 inches in between each cookie. Bake for 9 to 11 minutes until the cookies are pale golden brown.
12. Remove from the oven and let the cookies cool on the sheet for about 30 seconds. Transfer to a wire rack and let cool completely. Store at room temperature in an airtight container for several days.

ICED BROWN BUTTER OATMEAL COOKIES

Makes about 18 cookies

PREP TIME: 10 minutes
BAKE TIME: 10 to 12 minutes
EQIPMENT: Medium skillet, baking sheet
Ingredients:
FOR THE COOKIES
- 1 cup (2 sticks) unsalted butter
- 1 cup packed light brown sugar
- ½ cup granulated sugar
- 2 teaspoons vanilla extract
- 2 eggs, at room temperature
- 2 cups all-purpose flour
- 2 cups old-fashioned rolled oats
- 1 teaspoon baking soda
- 1 teaspoon ground cinnamon
- ¼ teaspoon salt

FOR THE ICING
- 1 cup powdered sugar
- 1 teaspoon vanilla extract
- 2 tablespoons low-fat or whole milk

Directions:

TO MAKE THE COOKIES

7. Preheat the oven to 350°F.

8. In a medium skillet set over medium heat, melt the butter and let it cook until it begins to foam, begins to brown, and smells toasty and nutty. Immediately remove the skillet from the heat and scrape the butter into a large bowl.

9. Add the brown sugar and granulated sugar. Using an electric mixer or wooden spoon, mix until well combined.

10. Add the vanilla and eggs, and beat until smooth.

11. Add the flour, oats, baking soda, cinnamon, and salt and beat until just combined. Drop the dough onto a baking sheet in heaping tablespoons, leaving about 2 inches between cookies. Bake for 10 to 12 minutes, until the cookies are golden brown around the edges.

12. Remove from the oven and let cool on the baking sheet for 2 to 3 minutes before transferring the cookies to a wire rack to cool completely. Store in an airtight container for up to 2 weeks.

TO MAKE THE ICING

2. In a medium bowl, stir together the powdered sugar, vanilla, and milk until smooth. Once the cookies have cooled for a few minutes, spoon the icing onto them, using about 2 teaspoons per cookie.

GINGER COOKIES

Makes about 24 cookies

PREP TIME: 10 minutes

BAKE TIME: 12 to 15 minutes

EQIPMENT: 2 baking sheets, medium bowl, large bowl

Ingredients:

- 1½ cups sugar, divided
- 2¼ cups all-purpose flour
- 2 teaspoons ground ginger
- 1 teaspoon ground cinnamon
- 1 teaspoon baking soda
- ½ teaspoon ground cloves
- ½ teaspoon salt
- ½ cup (1 stick) unsalted butter, at room temperature
- ⅓ cup molasses
- 1 egg

Directions:

7. Preheat the oven to 375°F.

8. Line 2 baking sheets with parchment paper, and put ½ cup of the sugar in a shallow bowl.

9. In a medium bowl, whisk the flour, ginger, cinnamon, baking soda, cloves, and salt.

10. In a large bowl, with a wooden spoon or electric mixer, cream together the butter and the remaining 1 cup of sugar.

11. Add the molasses and egg and continue to beat until the dough lightens. Add the dry ingredients and mix until thoroughly incorporated. With your hands, form the dough into 1-inch balls. Roll each ball in the bowl of sugar to coat lightly. Arrange the dough balls 2 inches apart on the prepared sheets. Bake for 12

to 15 minutes until the cookies are cracked and golden brown.

12. Remove from the oven and let the cookies cool on the baking sheet for 5 minutes before transferring them to a wire rack to cool completely. Store in an airtight container for up to 2 weeks.

CHOCOLATE–PEANUT BUTTER COOKIES

Makes about 50 cookies

PREP TIME: 10 minutes
SETTING TIME: 30 minutes
EQIPMENT: Baking sheet, medium saucepan
Ingredients:

- 2 cups sugar
- ½ cup low-fat or whole milk
- ½ cup (1 stick) unsalted butter
- ¼ cup unsweetened cocoa powder
- 3 cups old-fashioned rolled oats
- 1 cup smooth peanut butter
- 1 tablespoon vanilla extract
- ¼ teaspoon salt

Directions:

4. Line a baking sheet with parchment paper.

5. In a medium saucepan set over medium heat, combine the sugar, milk, butter, and cocoa powder. Bring to a boil, stirring occasionally. Let the mixture boil for 1 minute and remove the pan from the heat.

6. Stir in the oats, peanut butter, vanilla, and salt until combined. Using a tablespoon, drop rounds of dough onto the prepared sheet. Let sit at room temperature until the mixture cools and hardens, about 30 minutes. Serve immediately or refrigerate in an airtight container for up to 1 week.

PEANUT BUTTER COOKIES

Makes about 18 cookies

PREP TIME: 10 minutes
COOK TIME: 12 minutes
EQIPMENT: Baking sheet
Ingredients:

- 1 cup sugar
- 1 cup peanut butter
- 1 egg

Directions:

5. Preheat the oven to 350°F.

6. In a medium bowl, stir together the sugar, peanut butter, and egg until well combined. Scoop heaping

tablespoons of dough onto an ungreased baking sheet. Using the tines of a fork, press down on each dough mound to flatten it and make a pattern on top. Turn the fork 90 degrees and press down again to form a crisscross pattern.

7. Bake for 12 minutes.

8. Remove from the oven and let cool on the baking sheet for about 2 minutes before transferring to a wire rack to cool completely. Store at room temperature in an airtight container for several days.

MAPLE PECAN DROP COOKIES

Makes about 50 cookies

PREP TIME: 10 minutes

SETTING TIME: 30 minutes

EQIPMENT: 2 baking sheets, medium saucepan, blender or food processor

Ingredients:

- Nonstick baking spray
- ½ cup unsalted butter, melted
- ½ cup pure maple syrup
- ¼ cup packed light brown sugar
- ½ teaspoon vanilla extract
- ¼ teaspoon salt
- 1 cup old-fashioned rolled oats, toasted
- 1 cup finely chopped pecans, toasted

Directions:

5. Line 2 baking sheets with parchment paper and mist with baking spray.

6. In a medium saucepan set over medium-high heat, combine the butter, maple syrup, and brown sugar. Bring to a boil. Cook for 3 minutes, stirring. Remove the pan from the heat and immediately stir in the vanilla and salt. Let cool for 3 minutes.

7. Put the oats in a blender or food processor and grind coarsely.

8. Add the ground oats and pecans to the butter mixture and stir to mix well. Using a tablespoon, drop rounds of dough onto the prepared sheets. Let sit at room temperature for 30 minutes to cool and harden. Serve immediately or store in an airtight container, separated by sheets of parchment, for up to 1 week.

WHITE CHOCOLATE CRISP COOKIES

Makes about 50 cookies

PREP TIME: 10 minutes

CHILLING TIME: 30 minutes

EQIPMENT: 2 baking sheets, microwave or double boiler

Ingredients:

- 2 cups crisped rice cereal
- 1 cup mini marshmallows
- ½ cup creamy peanut butter

- 1 pound chopped white chocolate, or white chocolate chips

Directions:

5. Line 2 baking sheets with parchment paper.

6. In a large bowl, stir together the cereal and marshmallows.

7. In a large microwave-safe bowl, combine the peanut butter and white chocolate. Microwave at 50 percent power, in 30-second intervals, stirring in between, until completely melted and smooth. Pour the mixture over the cereal and marshmallows and stir to coat completely.

8. Using a tablespoon, drop the mixture on the prepared sheets. Refrigerate until the chocolate sets, about 30 minutes. Serve immediately or refrigerate in an airtight container, separated by sheets of parchment, for up to 1 week.

GOOEY CHOCOLATE BROWNIES

Makes 16 brownies

PREP TIME: 5 minutes

COOK TIME: 30 to 35 minutes

EQIPMENT: 8-inch square baking pan

Ingredients:

- ½ cup (1 stick) unsalted butter, plus more for preparing the pan, at room temperature

- 2 ounces unsweetened chocolate, finely chopped

- 2 eggs, at room temperature

- 1 teaspoon vanilla extract

- 1 cup sugar

- ¼ cup all-purpose flour

- ¼ teaspoon salt

Directions:

1. Preheat the oven to 325°F.

2. Generously grease an 8-inch square baking pan with butter.

3. Either in a saucepan set over medium heat or in a microwave-safe bowl, combine the butter and chocolate. Heat, or microwave at 50 percent power, in 30-second intervals, until both are completely melted and the mixture is smooth. Remove from the heat and set aside to cool for several minutes.

4. In a large bowl, whisk the butter-chocolate mixture with the eggs and vanilla until incorporated.

5. Add the sugar, flour, and salt and stir to mix well. Transfer the batter to the prepared pan and bake for 30 to 35 minutes.

6. Remove from the oven and let cool before cutting the brownies into bars. Serve immediately or store in an airtight container at room temperature for up to 5 days.

CHOCOLATE BROWNIES

Makes 16 brownies

PREP TIME: 10 minutes

CHILLING TIME: 3 hours

EQIPMENT: 9-inch square baking pan

Ingredients:

- Nonstick baking spray
- 1 (14-ounce) can sweetened condensed milk
- 2 ounces unsweetened chocolate, finely chopped
- 2½ cups graham cracker crumbs

Directions:

4. Spray a 9-inch square baking pan with baking spray.
5. In a medium saucepan set over medium-low heat, combine the sweetened condensed milk and chocolate. Cook for about 10 minutes, stirring constantly, until the chocolate is completely melted and the mixture is smooth. Remove the pan from the heat.
6. Add the graham cracker crumbs to the saucepan and stir to mix well. Transfer the mixture to the prepared baking pan and spread it into an even layer. Place the pan in the refrigerator and chill for at least 3 hours until well set. Slice into bars and serve chilled or refrigerate, covered, for up to 1 week.

MEXICAN COCONUT CANDY SQUARES

Makes 64 (1-inch) candies

PREP TIME: 10 minutes
CHILLING TIME: 1 hour
EQIPMENT: 8-inch square baking pan
Ingredients:

- 2 egg whites, lightly beaten
- 2 cups powdered sugar
- 1 cup shredded, unsweetened coconut
- ½ teaspoon vanilla extract
- 1 cup coconut oil
- Red or pink food coloring, for coloring the candies

Directions:

6. Line an 8-inch square baking pan with parchment paper.
7. In a medium bowl, stir together the beaten egg whites, powdered sugar, shredded coconut, and vanilla.
8. In a small saucepan set over low heat, melt the coconut oil. Stir the melted coconut oil into the sugar-and-coconut mixture. Transfer half the mixture to the prepared pan, pressing it down and smoothing the top into an even layer.
9. Add a few drops of food coloring to the remaining mixture and stir to blend the color. Pour the pink mixture on top of the mixture in the pan and press down, smoothing the top. Refrigerate for at least 1 hour until completely set.
10. Cut into 1-inch squares to serve.

NECTARINE GALETTE

Serves 6

PREP TIME: 10 minutes
COOK TIME: 12 to 15 minutes

EQIPMENT: Baking sheet, pastry brush

Ingredients:

- 1 uncooked 9-inch piecrust (homemade or store-bought)
- 4 to 5 ripe nectarines, cut into wedges
- 3 tablespoons sugar, divided
- 1 tablespoon cornstarch
- 1 egg, beaten

Directions:

7. Preheat the oven to 425°F.
8. Line a baking sheet with parchment paper and lay the piecrust out on the prepared sheet.
9. In a medium bowl, toss together the nectarine slices, 2 tablespoons of sugar, and the cornstarch. Transfer the mixture to a colander over the sink and let it drain for a few minutes. Pour the fruit onto the piecrust, mounding it in the center and leaving a 2-inch border of crust all the way around the fruit.
10. Fold the uncovered sides of the crust up over the edges of the fruit and fold into pleats to make a rustic circle.
11. Brush the beaten egg over the crust and sprinkle the remaining tablespoon of sugar over the crust. Bake for 12 to 15 minutes until the crust is golden brown.
12. Remove from the oven and let cool. Serve warm or at room temperature.

CANNOLI CREAM–FILLED MINI TARTLETS

Makes 24 mini tartlets

PREP TIME: 20 minutes
COOK TIME: 11 to 13 minutes
CHILLING TIME: 30 minutes
EQIPMENT: 24-cup mini muffin tin, 2½-inch round cookie cutter

Ingredients:

- All-purpose flour, for dusting the work surface
- 1 uncooked 9-inch piecrust (homemade or store-bought)
- 12 ounces whole-milk ricotta cheese, drained
- 8 ounces mascarpone cheese
- ½ cup plus 2 tablespoons powdered sugar, plus more for dusting
- ½ cup mini semisweet chocolate chips

Directions:

9. Preheat the oven to 400°F.
10. On a lightly floured surface, roll out the piecrust to an even thickness of about ⅛ inch.
11. Using a 2½-inch round cookie cutter, cut out 24 dough circles. Fit the dough circles into the cups of a mini muffin tin, pressing them in to form little dough cups. Bake for 11 to 13 minutes until lightly golden brown. Transfer the cups to a wire rack to cool completely.
12. While the cups cool, make the filling. In a large bowl, with a rubber spatula, stir together the ricotta and mascarpone cheeses until well combined and smooth.

13. Add the powdered sugar and stir to incorporate well.

14. Stir in the chocolate chips and mix well. Cover and refrigerate for at least 30 minutes.

15. When ready to fill the cups, transfer the filling to a piping bag or a resealable plastic bag with the tip cut off one bottom corner. Pipe the filling into the pastry cups.

16. Dust with powdered sugar and serve. Cover and refrigerate any leftovers for up to 3 days.

CHOCOLATE–PEANUT BUTTER TART

Serves 6

PREP TIME: 20 minutes

CHILLING TIME: 2 hours

EQIPMENT: 9-inch round tart or cake pan

Ingredients:

FOR THE CRUST

- 10 graham crackers, crushed (about 2 cups)
- 6 tablespoons (¾ stick) unsalted butter, melted

FOR THE FILLING

- 3 ounces milk chocolate, chopped, plus more to make chocolate curls for garnish
- 1¼ cups heavy (whipping) cream, divided
- ¾ cup creamy peanut butter
- 4 ounces cream cheese, at room temperature
- ⅓ cup sweetened condensed milk

Directions:

TO MAKE THE CRUST

1. In a medium bowl, stir together the graham cracker crumbs and butter until thoroughly combined. Press the mixture into the bottom and up the sides of a 9-inch round tart or cake pan. Refrigerate the crust while you prepare the filling.

TO MAKE THE FILLING

1. In a medium microwave-safe bowl, combine the chocolate and ½ cup of cream. Microwave at 50 percent power, in 30-second intervals, stirring in between, until the chocolate is completely melted and the mixture is smooth. Let cool, whisking occasionally. Once cool and thick, spread the chocolate ganache into the bottom of the prepared crust in an even layer. Refrigerate the crust again until ready to add the peanut butter filling.

2. In a medium bowl, stir together the peanut butter, cream cheese, and sweetened condensed milk.

3. In a large bowl, using a handheld electric mixer or in a stand mixer fitted with the whisk attachment, whip the remaining ¾ cup of cream until it holds soft peaks. Gently fold the whipped cream into the peanut butter mixture. Spread the mixture in the crust on top of the chocolate layer, smoothing the top with a rubber spatula. Return the filled tart to the refrigerator for at least 2 hours until set.

4. Garnish the chilled tart with chocolate curls, slice into wedges, and serve.

PEAR CUSTARD TART

Serves 6

PREP TIME: 5 minutes

COOK TIME: 20 to 30 minutes

EQIPMENT: 9-inch round cake pan

Ingredients:

- ¾ cup (1½ sticks) unsalted butter, plus more for preparing the cake pan
- ⅓ cup all-purpose flour
- 1½ cups powdered sugar, plus more for dusting
- 1 cup almond meal
- 3 eggs, beaten
- 3 pears, cored and cut into wedges

Directions:

1. Preheat the oven to 400°F.
2. Lightly grease a 9-inch round cake pan.
3. In a small saucepan set over medium heat, melt the butter and cook for about 3 minutes until it just turns golden brown. Remove from the heat and let cool.
4. Meanwhile, in a medium bowl, stir together the flour, powdered sugar, and almond meal.
5. Add the melted butter and the eggs and stir to combine thoroughly. Pour the batter into the prepared pan and arrange the pear wedges on top. Bake for 15 minutes, lower the heat to 350°F, then bake for 5 to 10 minutes more, until just golden brown.
6. Dust with powdered sugar, slice into wedges, and serve warm or at room temperature.

DOUBLE CHOCOLATE GANACHE TART

Serves 6

PREP TIME: 15 minutes

COOK TIME: 20 minutes

CHILLING TIME: 1 hour

EQIPMENT: 9-inch tart pan with a removable bottom

Ingredients:

- 32 chocolate wafer cookies (about 8 ounces), crushed into fine crumbs (I prefer Nabisco Famous Chocolate Wafers)
- 2 tablespoons sugar
- ½ teaspoon salt
- 6 tablespoons (¾ stick) unsalted butter, melted
- 12 ounces semisweet chocolate, chopped
- 1¼ cups heavy (whipping) cream
- Lightly sweetened whipped cream, for serving
- 1½ cups fresh raspberries

Directions:

1. Preheat the oven to 350°F.
2. In a medium bowl, stir together the cookie crumbs, sugar, and salt.
3. Stir in the melted butter and mix until well combined. Press the cookie-crumb mixture into the bottom and up the sides of a 9-inch tart pan with a removable bottom. Bake for 20 minutes.
4. Remove from the oven and let cool.
5. In a medium microwave-safe bowl, combine the chocolate and cream. Microwave at 50 percent power, in 30-second intervals, stirring in between, until the chocolate is completely melted and the mixture is smooth. Pour the chocolate mixture into the prepared crust. Refrigerate for at least 1 hour until set.
6. Serve chilled, cut into wedges, and garnished with whipped cream and raspberries

RASPBERRY PIE SQUARES

Makes 16 squares

PREP TIME: 20 minutes

COOKING TIME: 10 minutes

CHILLING TIME: 3 hours, 30 minutes

EQIPMENT: 8-inch square baking pan, blender or food processor

Ingredients:

FOR THE CRUST

- 1½ cups finely ground graham cracker crumbs (from about 9 graham crackers)
- ⅓ cup sugar
- 6 tablespoons (¾ stick) unsalted butter, melted

FOR THE FILLING

- 2 tablespoons water
- 2¼ teaspoons (1 envelope) unflavored gelatin
- 3 cups fresh raspberries, divided
- ½ cup sugar
- ¼ cup cream cheese, at room temperature
- 2 tablespoons low-fat or whole milk
- 1 tablespoon powdered sugar

Directions:

TO MAKE THE CRUST

4. Preheat the oven to 375°F.
5. In a medium bowl, stir together the graham cracker crumbs, sugar, and butter until well combined. Press the mixture into the bottom of an 8-inch baking pan in an even layer. Bake for about 7 minutes until lightly browned.
6. Remove from the oven and let cool.

TO MAKE THE FILLING

7. Put the water in a small bowl and sprinkle the gelatin over it. Let rest, stirring occasionally, until the gelatin fully dissolves. Prepare an ice bath by filling a large bowl with water and ice.
8. Meanwhile, in a blender or food processor, purée all but ½ cup of the raspberries until smooth. Transfer the purée to a medium saucepan set over medium heat.

9. Add the sugar and bring to a boil.

10. Add the gelatin mixture and cook for about 1 minute, stirring. Transfer the raspberry mixture to a medium bowl and set the bowl in the ice bath. Transfer the ice bath with the filling mixture to the refrigerator and chill for about 30 minutes, stirring once in a while with a rubber spatula, until the mixture is cool and thick.

11. While the raspberry mixture chills, in a medium bowl, combine the cream cheese, milk, and powdered sugar and, using an electric mixer or wooden spoon, beat until very smooth.

12. Spread the chilled raspberry filling over the prepared graham cracker crust and spoon the cream cheese mixture on top, placing dollops all over. Drag a knife through the cream cheese mixture to swirl it with the raspberry mixture. Top with the reserved raspberries. Refrigerate for about 3 hours, until fully set. Cut into 16 squares and serve chilled. Cover any leftovers with plastic wrap and refrigerate for up to 3 days.

VANILLA ICE CREAM

Serves 8

PREP TIME: 10 minutes

CHILLING AND FREEZING TIME: 4 hours

EQIPMENT: Freezer-safe storage container

Ingredients:

- 1 cup whole milk
- ¾ cup granulated sugar
- Pinch salt
- 2 cups heavy (whipping) cream
- 1 tablespoon vanilla extract

Directions:

5. In a medium bowl, combine the milk, sugar, and salt. Whisk, or use an electric mixer to beat, for about 3 minutes until the sugar dissolves.

6. Add the cream and vanilla and stir to mix. Refrigerate for at least 1 hour.

7. Pour the mixture into a freezer-safe storage container, cover with plastic wrap, and freeze for about 45 minutes before checking on it the first time. As soon as it begins to freeze around the edges, mix it vigorously with a whisk, spatula, wooden spoon, or ideally, a handheld electric mixer or immersion blender. Continue to freeze, mixing it every 30 minutes, until it is fully frozen, about 3 hours total.

8. Keep frozen until ready to serve.

GOOEY CHOCOLATE BROWNIES

Makes 16 brownies

PREP TIME: 5 minutes

COOK TIME: 30 to 35 minutes

EQIPMENT: 8-inch square baking pan

Ingredients:

- ½ cup (1 stick) unsalted butter, plus more for preparing the pan, at room temperature

- 2 ounces unsweetened chocolate, finely chopped
- 2 eggs, at room temperature
- 1 teaspoon vanilla extract
- 1 cup sugar
- ¼ cup all-purpose flour
- ¼ teaspoon salt

Directions:

7. Preheat the oven to 325°F.
8. Generously grease an 8-inch square baking pan with butter.
9. Either in a saucepan set over medium heat or in a microwave-safe bowl, combine the butter and chocolate. Heat, or microwave at 50 percent power, in 30-second intervals, until both are completely melted and the mixture is smooth. Remove from the heat and set aside to cool for several minutes.
10. In a large bowl, whisk the butter-chocolate mixture with the eggs and vanilla until incorporated.
11. Add the sugar, flour, and salt and stir to mix well. Transfer the batter to the prepared pan and bake for 30 to 35 minutes.
12. Remove from the oven and let cool before cutting the brownies into bars. Serve immediately or store in an airtight container at room temperature for up to 5 days.

MOLTEN CHOCOLATE LAVA CAKES

Serves 4

PREP TIME: 10 minutes
COOK TIME: 12 to 14 minutes
EQIPMENT: 4 (6-ounce) ramekins or custard cups

Ingredients:

- Nonstick baking spray
- ½ cup (1 stick) unsalted butter
- 4 ounces semisweet chocolate, chopped
- 1¼ cups powdered sugar, plus more for garnish
- 3 egg yolks
- 2 eggs
- 1 teaspoon vanilla extract
- ½ cup all-purpose flour

Directions:

9. Preheat the oven to 425°F.
10. Spray 4 (6-ounce) ramekins or custard cups with nonstick baking spray and place them on a baking sheet.
11. In a large microwave-safe bowl, combine the butter and chocolate. Microwave at 50 percent power for about 1 minute until the butter melts. Whisk until the chocolate is completely melted and the mixture is smooth.
12. Add the powdered sugar and stir to combine.
13. In a small bowl, whisk the egg yolks and eggs and add them to the chocolate mixture along with the

vanilla. Stir the batter to combine thoroughly.

14. Add the flour and stir to mix. Scoop the batter into the prepared ramekins, dividing equally. Transfer the baking sheet with the filled ramekins to the oven and bake for 12 to 14 minutes until the edges are firm, but the centers are still soft.

15. Remove from the oven and let cool for 1 minute. Run a sharp knife around the inside of each ramekin and then invert each onto a serving plate.

16. Dust the tops with powdered sugar and serve immediately.

LEMON CHEESECAKE

Serves 10

PREP TIME: 15 minutes

CHILLING TIME: 5 hours

EQIPMENT: Electric mixer, 9-inch springform pan

Ingredients:

- 1½ cups finely ground graham cracker crumbs (from about 9 graham crackers)
- ¼ cup packed brown sugar
- 6 tablespoons (¾ stick) unsalted butter, melted
- 1 cup heavy (whipping) cream
- 8 ounces cream cheese, at room temperature
- ½ cup lemon curd
- ⅓ cup powdered sugar
- 1 teaspoon vanilla extract

Directions:

6. In a medium bowl, stir together the graham cracker crumbs, brown sugar, and butter until well combined. Press the mixture into the bottom and a bit up the sides of a 9-inch springform pan in an even layer. Refrigerate for 1 hour.

7. In a large bowl, using a handheld electric mixer or in a stand mixer, whip the cream until it holds stiff peaks.

8. In another large bowl, beat the cream cheese until it is creamy and smooth.

9. Beat the lemon curd, powdered sugar, and vanilla into the cream cheese.

10. Using a rubber spatula, gently fold in the whipped cream. Spoon the mixture into the prepared crust and use the rubber spatula to smooth the top. Refrigerate for at least 4 hours until completely set. Serve chilled.